UNCOVERING YOUR WORTH:
FROM LEGAL CUSTODY TO UCLA

CHRISTIAN D. GREEN

CONFESSIONS PUBLISHING

Uncovering Your Worth: From Legal Custody to UCLA
Copyright © 2019 by Christian D. Green
ISBN: 978-0-692-10996-0

Printed and bound in the United States of America.

Editor: Erick Markley
Cover Design and Cover Layout: Joshua Wirth
Photographer: Charles Jones

Confessions Publishing is a subsidiary of Roszien Kay LLC, Lancaster, CA 93536
For information regarding discounts on bulk purchase and all other inquiries, please contact the author directly at uncoveringyourworth@gmail.com or 661-714-0616.

This memoir is dedicated to the loving memory of my grandparents Mrs. Geraldine Cromwell and Mr. Herbert Cromwell. Especially to my Grandmother- Mother Cromwell. Also, to my biological mother Denise Carter and father whose identity is still unknown. And to the entire Cromwell, Green, Carter, Dorris, Mt. Sac, UCLA and LFC Family.

Without all of your contributions, I would not be the success I am today.

Thank you.

un·cov·er

/ˌənˈkəvər/

verb

1. remove a cover or covering from.
2. "he uncovered the face of the dead man"

1. *synonyms:*
   1. expose, reveal, lay bare;
   2. unwrap, unveil;
   3. strip, denude
   4. "she uncovered the new artwork"

   ○ discover (something previously secret or unknown).
   ○ "further evidence has been uncovered"

   ○ *synonyms:*
      ○ detect, discover, come across, stumble on, chance on, find, turn up, unearth, dig up;More

CONTENTS

INTRODUCTION

Imagine being in Paris, France on a study abroad trip. You are with 60 other students and some small fragile red-headed white woman says, "why would anyone want to read anything about you?! Who are you? I have been doing this for years! What do you have to offer?"

What would you do?
What could you say?

Well, this happened to me. I remember it like it was yesterday. My sister Krystal and I were sitting at the table with this lady and her husband, our study abroad guides, trying escargot (snails) for the first time. We were conversing about European and American politics, culture and our future endeavors.

When the lady said her words, it seemed like it was a question and statement combined. To be quite honest her words made me angry. Mainly because, according to my family and friends, I sometimes wear my emotions on my sleeves.

But to be quite frank, when people question my abilities, it makes me hungry to prove a point. Her words made me doubt my narrative, but it also pushed me to write this book. Right then I knew I would have to share my story. In that moment I knew I had what it took to do it. In that moment it hit me, it was true what my Pastor and foster brother Darrell always said, "What you need to make it, is already in you." My story and my voice were built for millions of others from a foster youth background to read and learn from.

It was while we were on a tour learning about the European political system that I realized what I had to do. We started off in London for a week, then caught the last fairy (because of the frequent train bombings that were happening in London at the time) to Amsterdam, Netherlands. We stayed there for four days, then took a charter bus to Brussels, Belgium for three days and then to Paris, France for ten days. This was by far one of the best experiences ever. It is actually the trip I like to tell all of my incoming transfers and students of color about. This is the trip I tell them about to emphasize the need to travel! Get out of California! Get out of the country! LIVE!

I didn't know this trip would not just be about learning international politics. But It would be more about finding and learning about myself. What I discovered was loving one's self and one's narrative is a lesson in itself. It's hard. It's hard to stop being critical of yourself. It's hard to get rid of regrets. It's hard to overturn past mistakes. And it's hard to truly appreciate one's flaws. It takes time.

It took me years to accept my narrative and flaws. Some of my biggest flaws are in plain sight. From my picture on the cover you can see: my hairline is crooked; I wear glasses; I have a big nose; my eyes are little, somewhat Asian (I guess ancestry.com was correct when they said I was two percent Asian descent); my ears are small; I have a shadow on my beard; and to be hundred (real) - my beard game is ugly, it is not the best. So yeah, these are some of my flaws that I share with you as the reader, but yet even in my imperfections, I am perfect. How can I (and you) not be perfect when made in the image of a perfect God according to Genesis 1:27? Because this is the case, we must learn to love ourselves.

Repeat after me: "I love myself."

Accepting and loving one's self is something that one must work on daily. From rich to poor, we all have insecurities, fears, complications, regrets and problems. But through time we learn confidence. One thing I tell all of my students and family members growing up, through life's obstacles and journey, we build our confidence, not arrogance. We build confidence to help us learn how to appreciate ourselves. It makes our road to building a life for ourselves and others of higher quality.

But during this building we ask God and ourselves many questions, such as; why did "this" happen? Why did you allow me to go through this? Why did you take my parents from me at an early age? Why did you allow me to be born in a prison?

I am here to tell you these questions are perfectly normal! Everyone has a "this!"

The "this" I am referring to can be multifaceted. It can be losing a parent or loved one. It can be financial problems. It can be entering the foster care system. It can be being molested. It can be no access to fulfilling your dreams and visions.

For me, I had a number of "this." At one point in my life, I blamed God and everyone else for the loss of my parents. I blamed them for being raised alone in a world where people said they loved me and it not being enough.

In this book I want to challenge each reader to think about what is their "this."
It is your duty to uncover your "this." We can receive advice from everyone: our moms, dads, brothers, sisters and friends, but until we, personally, uncover it, the value of it will never be appreciated at the level it produces radical change. I want everyone to know through this book that their "this" is something that can and will add value and worth to their story.

We all have a story. What is yours?

Lets us go down a quick journey, my journey.….

I was born in a prison. This was something that I didn't know of until after I was eighteen. I thought my grandmother was my blood. I thought my cousins and the ones I grew up with were my blood. However, this was false. As a result, I always internally asked myself whether my parents wanted me? And because I am bi-racial, I started questioning my Blackness. These questions were a byproduct of not knowing my true identity.

Every day, captured with wonderings of - what my maternal mother was thinking when she had me?
Did she not care?
Did she know who my father was but did not want to tell anyone?
Was she raped in jail?
How were the doctors toward my mother at my birth?
How did she feel after conceiving me?
Did she even hold me in her arms when she had me?

In this book, I want everyone to learn through my experiences to accept and learn from their own experiences. Learning from your own experiences will add value to your worth. Value is defined as "the regard that something is held to deserve; the importance, worth, or usefulness of something." Some synonyms of value are worth, usefulness, advantage, profit, good and benefit. Uncover is defined "as to reveal and to discover." When you think of those that excavate historical items, it takes them time, it takes years, months and days to uncover the first bone or skull. As with our life, it will take time to truly uncover and appreciate our life experiences. This is radical.

As a motivational speaker, sociologist, activist, advocate, professor, teacher, pastor and community member, I want this book to inspire and challenge everyone that reads these words to go after their dreams! You must ask yourself why did God show me this? What is the importance of this? This book will use scripture, locations, geography, pictures, poetry, and activities to inspire you to think critically about your experiences in life and understand that that in itself is a contribution to research.

As a young biracial Black male, I had to encounter a lot of issues that the Black community and society in general does not talk about. In this book, I will highlight central themes surrounding, but not limited to: Blackness, agency, resistance, vulnerability, racism, foster care system, place, location, migration, and changing and expanding narratives through radical pedagogy. Though this is a short book, which is intentional, there will be activities throughout the book to help you write down your flaws, memories, goals and action steps to truly help you to uncover your worth. I will also conclude with my top ten tips of navigating collegiate spaces.

I pray that you are blessed through this book. I pray you arrive at the understanding that in order to reach the promise, you have to appreciate the process!

Now Let's Uncover your flaws: When you look in the mirror what do you see? Open your camera app on your phone right now and look at YOU! What do you see? What don't you like?

Write down your flaws?

What do you like when you see your image?

Why do you think it's important to notice and appreciate our flaws?

_____

_____

_____

_____

_____

_____

_____

_____

_____

_____

_____

_____

_____

_____

Uncovering your flaws will help you to appreciate your narrative!

PART I

CHAPTER 1:

SACRAMENTO, CA

Being confident of this very thing, that he which hath begun a good work in you will perform it until the day of Jesus Christ:- Philippians 1:6

According to kidsdata.org, 6.8% of Sacramento county are of foster youth demographic.

I had enough. Being caught up in a cycle of living from house to house. Going from one club to the next. Indulging in drugs, alcohol, sex work and being around the wrong crowd. I was on the run from God and from my purpose. Not truly understanding my worth.

I felt trapped. I had been intertwined with sex, drugs, alcohol and violence for too long. I loved going to the clubs. I loved going to "turn up" with my bros, my best friends and my sistahs, but I knew there was more to my worth. After constant conversations with friends of "oooh chile last night was too crazy," or "I can't believe I blacked out like that!" or "did you see how he/she was looking at you?" or "She wanted you" or "where was my wallet and how did I lose my phone, again?" I knew there was more value to my life. I knew my grandmother wouldn't have wanted this lifestyle to take me out. So, I left Los Angeles, California to head up north, to "Sac-town" (Sacramento, CA).

My sister, Tameka said, "Yes! Please come to Sacramento, come give it a try! We would love to have you." Not fully understanding what it would mean to live with her and my eight nieces and nephews at the time, I decided to up and leave. I couldn't find a job in Lancaster, California for over a year, so what other option was there? I was 21, with no options, something had to give. I knew there was more.

My move to Sacramento in 2008 was a decision that changed my life for the better. It was one of the best decisions I could have ever made. After being in Sacramento for only two weeks, I finally got a job at California Storage Center. Yes, you know the places where people store their hoardings, their family heirlooms, their artwork, their furniture, their collections of old cds and dvds, and for some, their junk.

California Storage Centers was an unforgettable experience. There, I gained an appreciation for country music, patience, hard-work, part-time work, Christ and schooling once again. Even though it was a part-time job, it was a job. Working there three days a week afforded me opportunities that I did not have previously. On the positive end, I was introduced to country music. On the negative end, there is where I would encounter my first taste of on the job racism.

Serving as the assistant manager with another Black male was fun, but also caused tension with us and our white boss. The storage center had a huge population of people of color (POC) tenants. Some would pay on time and some just could not afford to save their possessions of personal value. It left this impression in the manager's head that all Black and Latinos were broke and could not afford to save or store their family belongings and valuables.

When families couldn't afford to save their belongings, the process was messy for everybody. Their family and personal treasures and belongings would be put up for auction. We would give them notices when it was past their third, tenth and thirtieth day of being late. After a certain amount of notices, the lien process followed. This process was a mess but allowed people to get the money needed. If they could not get it in time, they would begin to rack up egregious amounts of fees. I learned this was another way an institution could keep the poor people poor.

I felt bad for the people. But my power was limited. Some would literally come in the day before or on the last day to pay. However, there were a few that was not so lucky. Most times, it would be again, people of color, but more specifically, Black folk.

One day, the head manager--the stereotypical white heteronormative patriarchal male he was--felt comfortable enough to say: "that nigger was supposed to do . . ." Now grant it, over time, it was building. I think my coworker and I were to blame for it though. He would make comments about Black people being late on payments. We would agree. We would agree with him when he would say the same about white people too. But I never called them a redneck or a cracker or any other racial pejorative. He would make comments about Black people not caring for their credit and we would agree. Shoot, we were still facing our own credit problems. He then proceeded to say, "those niggers . . ." After this, my Black colleague and I were lost on what to do. How do you handle a hidden racist? How do you deal with someone that has become a friend, but crossed the racial lines? Well, long story short, I ended up writing a long letter to the corporate headquarters and moved to a bigger and a more secure job: Blue Shield of California.

On the final day at the storage center, the head of the company and his lawyer took my coworker and I out to a restaurant. The outing seemed like a normal conversation about what they could do to help the problem die down. Even in that situation, I did not know I had the power to ask for more than just my last two weeks of pay. I did not understand what I was truly worth...Millions.

After leaving the storage center, I joined the healthcare industry. I was in the middle of class at Sacramento City College when I got the call from Blue Shield of California that I got the job. I disenrolled from school immediately. It was a hard decision, but I had to hold off on school for one more semester.

The healthcare industry was something I was not too familiar with. Thankfully, my resume said I was an expert in the customer service field. I landed a great job with great benefits as a customer service representative. I was excited and relieved at the same time because finding a job as a young Black male was hard to do. This customer service job gave me the opportunity I so desperately needed. The fact of the matter was that I was transitioning from my foster family home and didn't have job resources available to me; or I lacked the knowledge that there were resources available to me.

As a result of this amazing job opportunity, I gained a plethora of great friends and a wealth of knowledge. I met my first godson, Khaaliq Baker, and his mom, Shalamonet Baker. I was trained by one of the best MMA Fighters today, Max Griffin. I gained some great longtime friends. I mean, *come on* !!! This was truly a step up from cleaning and sweeping out storage units. Here, I had my own desk, my own computer, my own phone and guess what? my own headset!

The benefits did not stop there. My health and dental were covered and school tuition reimbursement was up to 75% of all costs. The healthcare and dental package was a huge plus for me because most older foster youth couldn't afford health care. And because Blue Shield allowed me to work and go to school, I re-enrolled in classes at the local community college. This customer service job truly helped me to provide a somewhat better life for myself, especially because my support system was not strong and I didn't have parentals to call on in troubling times. Unfortunately, this lack is the reality of life of most foster youth.

Blue Shield afforded me the opportunity to move into my first apartment, Folsom Lake Ranch Condominiums. It was right down the street from Folsom Prison. It seemed like the idea of being locked up or surrounded by a "prison" would follow me everywhere I went. Yet, I thought I made it. I had my own car, I had my own home (an apartment I was renting) and I had my own money. I was I-N-D-E-P-E-N-D-E-N-T. The apartments even had wild turkeys walking in the hills which was my own backyard. It was peaceful.

However, as perfect as it seemed, it still had its downside. It was located thirty minutes from my family and church family. Nevertheless, I made it work. It was a one bedroom with a den and a balcony. It was fabulous in my eyes; no one could tell me nothing. I lived there for a year until my lease was up and then moved to Sacramento near Sacramento State and near the church I attended.

I had it good during this time period. But I was hiding behind the phones. I hid behind the phones for several reasons. One reason was because there was no face to face action. I was a customer service agent that handled the appeals, complaints, grievances and claim calls of our customers at the "Shield." I really enjoyed this! I loved helping people. As far as I was concerned I was fulfilling my love even though this was a different form of helping.

Although I really loved helping people as a customer service agent, I used my position to hide my insecurities. I was insecure because I had a chipped tooth and a gut, and I wasn't too confident with my appearance. Have you ever felt that way? I was also insecure because I was small, and I was never the gym rat (and still am not).

At the age of 11, I was running in the bathroom at Sizzler, I slipped and fell, chipped my front left tooth and pushed three of my teeth back. At that time instead of making a complaint to the restaurant manager, I did nothing. The adults in my life did nothing... I just emerged from the floor with my chipped pushed back teeth. Our inaction is something that I reflect on now... I wish I had known a lawyer back then because maybe we could have probably sued... The bottom line is I *should* have received compensation for what had happened to me. But again, most foster youth do not have access to these resources, especially legal ones.

Despite my insecurities and my hiding, Sacramento was a blessing. Not only because of Blue Shield of California, but also because I made an attempt to change my life, while not even knowing or intending to. I made a plan that worked. This unexpected plan prepared me for my next journey.

Although the above had been the case, I had my shares of ups and downs. I went from being a customer service representative, to my final job within the company as an appeals coordinator. During this time, I had one boss, Stacey, that would work my nerves. I was the youngest one on her team. But everyone loved me. So much so that they would stop by my cubicle to say hi, and to check in on me and ask for advice. During that time, I thought of myself as a socialite. On average, I had more visitors than Stacey had. This fact alone may have caused her to become jealousy, but I am unsure.

What I am sure of is that she harbored negative feelings towards me. Stacey felt like I did not go over and beyond for her. Which wasn't true at all. The fact of the matter was that the department we worked in was more of data entry. As a result, it became heavily repetitious and annoying. So much so that it was easy for you to become bored and to even fall asleep. I remember one time, I was at the desk trying my hardest to stay awake, but I fell asleep for about 5-10 minutes. I sat there unknowingly asleep until Stacey came over and tapped me on the shoulder. Once I woke up, she asked me to meet her in her office. After gathering myself I went to her. Inside her office, Stacey said "if you want to sleep you can go home, we cannot have this here." Thankfully, she did not send me home, but she always kept her eye on me.

It wasn't difficult for Stacey to keep an eye on me either. I sat right in front of her desk. After the close encounter I had with her about falling asleep, I knew that I had to be on my best behavior. Now, every time I would look behind me I caught her looking directly at me. It was as if she was waiting for me to mess up. It was an unbelievable feeling. I knew I *had* to leave.

Being in that cubicle made me feel inferior, less than, always watched and always under surveillance. It became too much for me. I needed out! So, I applied to between eight to ten jobs outside of her department. Fortunately for me, I got hired as an appeals coordinator. Because I was no longer underneath Stacey, I was moved out of her department into the other department as a claims processor for children with autism.

Although this new position was great, I continued to experience difficulties. My new set of co-workers would monitor everything I would do. Because of this continued annoyance and stress, I knew I had to leave this department too.

I had been there for 4.5 years. Even though this was the case, no upper management job would hire me. I had no degree, no formal education and not enough experience. I knew there had to be more for me than working a dead end 9-5. So, I prayed and fasted about what to do, and I left; back to Los Angeles, the place I had originally ran from.

The fact still remained, Blue Shield allowed me to take care of my older niece and nephew that was facing some issues within our family. It allowed me to take care of myself with no leaning on others. God had finally provided for me; at least that's what I had thought. It allowed me to understand that there was more to my worth beyond what I could imagine.

Now Let's Uncover your goals

Everyone has them. But one reason why there is no delivery is because of the failure to write down a clear plan. List your goals.

Write down your 6 month plan

Write down your 1 year plan

Write down your 3 year plan

Write down your 10 year plan

Writing down, reflecting on, and implementing your goals will lead to you completing them.

CHAPTER 2:
SAN BERNARDINO, CA

———————◆———————

When my father and my mother forsake me, then the LORD will take me up. - Psalms 27:10

According to kidsdata.org, 8.3 % of San Bernardino County youth are of foster youth demographic.

It was the second stop on my "home alone" Christmas winter tour across the United States: Houston, Texas, where my life would change. My tour included first stopping to visit my brother Steddy in Dallas, Texas, because I just love Dallas (#teampappadeaux). Then, I went to New York City to live my "home alone" experience while making a visit to the newly built African American Museum in D.C. (Shoutout to Chris' aunt that hooked us up with free tickets).

From Dallas Texas, I took the megabus to Houston to visit my sister/cousin, Myesha, her husband, Adrian, my aunt Tracey, and her domestic partner Quintin; and most importantly, the newest addition to the family: Amiyah Richardson. I loved going to visit them because it always reminded me of the good times with my grandmother and all the beautiful memories we had growing up.

My aunt had recently retired and bought a house on the lake (can we say *gorgeous!*). Because she has always had a knack for interior designing, she designed it to be a place of rest and comfort. As we relaxed and while we were talking about family and growing up without parents, I remember the conversation starting with "how does it feel not having any parents? I have never really asked you." We were sitting in the living room, Myesha, aunt Tracey and myself. I begin to feel anxiety and mixed emotions. She was right. We had never talked about something like that.

So, I proceeded to tell her how I've learned to cope with it. I had a great support system with my grandmother, her mom and dad being there to play the role. I told her how I sometimes felt out of place, isolated and alone because when I would play sports, or do events, my mom and dad were not too involved because of their age; which I knew I couldn't blame them for. They raised their children already. Although this had been the case, when I would see my friends with their parents and families, I felt jealousy, sadness, anger and hatred. I would ask God what were my parents like? Why did he allow them not to be in my life?

I think these feelings of loneliness was the reason why I acted out to gain attention. I was always a smart kid, but I wanted my parents. I wanted to know what it was to have an involved mom and dad.

After making these statements, I asked my aunt what happened on that day. My aunt told me I was born in a prison. No, this is not a joke. I was born in San Bernardino County Jail to an incarcerated mother that did not know what to do. Impacted by the War on Drugs and War on Poverty by President Lyndon B Johnson down through Reaganomics in the 1980's. She became heavily involved in drugs and sex. And I fell victim to her skeletons.

Over that winter break, aunt Tracey calmly said, "child, we did not know what to expect. I remember being right there when we got the call. The telephone rang, and I answered, and it said you had a collect call from …. I said Mom its Denise, she's in jail, you want me to say yes? She said yes! She told mom that if you want him to come get him!"

After she told me that news, I felt empowered to know that my grandmother wanted me.

Initially they thought I was just a light skinned Black baby, but as I grew older my hair texture was different and my features were different. They knew that I was not from the same cloth as the father that was listed on my birth certificate. My grandmother was the mother of the father on my birth certificate. She was not even my blood. But she still never gave up on me or gave me to the system. Even though some may be upset to have found out that they had been lied to for so many years, I wasn't. It was like I gained a sense of closure.

This closure led me to understanding more of my worth.

How could I not be thankful or appreciative towards a family who took me in when they were not even of my blood relations. God knew what he was doing. He knew what it would take to build me into the man I am today - an unapologetically loving family.

Although I have no knowledge as to whether or not I take after my birth parents, I'd like to think I take after my mom (my grandmother), Mrs. Geraldine Cromwell, or, as some of the church folk knew her, Mother Cromwell. She was a loving, selfless, caring, nurturing, empowering and phenomenal woman. She is the reason why I write this book. She raised me, nurtured me, cared for me and dedicated herself and her resources to my wellbeing. She did this even though my biological mother gave up. So that I won't beat myself up over this, I like to think that maybe Denise Carter wasn't ready.

Mother Cromwell was and is a huge reason of my success and who I am today (*Pause, can you identify someone that played a huge role in your life?*) Unfortunately, during my sophomore year of high school, I lost the only mother I knew, my grandmother. Imagine being a teenager and losing someone you loved and knew since birth. The person that stepped in and played the role of your mother. This can and is one of the most painful experiences. Truthfully, only those who have lost someone, know the hurt one must endure as a result of that.

I think about her every day. I think about what if she were still alive today? How would our family be if she were still alive? Have you ever lost someone? Have you ever cared or been cared for by someone and then lost them all of a sudden? It is painful to say the least.

As painful as it was and still is for me, my early memories help to ease the pain. During the early years of my life, we lived in San Bernardino. I only vaguely remember anything about San Bernardino because I was only there from the time I was two days old until 4 years old. 2564 St. Elmo Dr. San Bernardino CA 92404, was the exact address. We ended up moving from San Bernardino because my grandmother and grandfather separated. He moved to Fresno because he spent summers there as a child and had family there.

When they reconciled and got back together, my grandmother moved to Fresno to be with him and took me, my cousins and my brother with her. I wish I had more time to talk to her about her journey. Like, why did she do that? How was it for her as a youngster with no family? Was this the reason for her holding on to us and not putting us into the system? I wish I could tell you so much more, but I can't because the answers to these questions went to the grave with her.

I'm not certain why my family didn't remain in San Bernardino once my grandparents reconciled. Perhaps it was because my grandparents must have known that nothing productive or of value was to come out of being in that environment. In the news today, we hear about how San Bernardino filed for bankruptcy and how there was a huge mass shooting. Even though this is the case or may have been the case even back then, there was still good there.

My grandfather's family, the Cromwell's lived there. My grandfather, Herbert Cromwell, had eight other siblings, so we would host family reunions and cookouts there. This was the best part of San Bernardino. Every time we would come back, his family remembered me because I was the "white/light skinned" boy that my grandfather had next to his hip. They loved me unconditionally too. Even though our family could be described as dysfunctional and society wants us to believe that dysfunctions is not a good thing, it is. No family is perfect. To put it simply, we cannot base our family ties upon society's beliefs and depictions.

Aside from my family still being in San Bernardino, there is a legendary and iconic restaurant that our family still visits today, called the Amapolo. This was mommy's favorite burrito spot. She loved their famous "hot spicy pork burrito." Every time we would go back for a family reunion she would ask for these same burritos to be brought back, so that she could save them for a rainy day. My memories of her demanding that those burritos be brought back to Fresno, is something I will never forget; mainly because I would steal half of it even though she hated that.

Now Let's Uncover family secrets

Have you ever discovered family secrets well after the time passed by? If so, how did you deal with them?

_____
_____
_____
_____
_____
_____
_____
_____
_____
_____
_____
_____
_____

If you haven't dealt with them, what's preventing you from it?

_____
_____
_____
_____
_____
_____
_____
_____
_____
_____
_____
_____

Who would you trust enough to help you with the process, and why?

_____
_____
_____
_____
_____
_____
_____
_____
_____
_____
_____
_____
_____
_____
_____
_____
_____
_____

We all have family secrets. Once they are revealed it's very important that we accept and process them!

CHAPTER 3:

FRESNO, CA

Train up a child in the way he should go: and when he is old, he will not depart from it. - Proverbs 22:6

According to kidsdata.org, 5.6 % of Fresno, California population are of the foster youth demographic.

Christmas 1996, everyone was there at big momma's house in Fresno, California. Mother Geraldine Cromwell was "Big Mama." If you have seen the movie Soul Food, you'd know who I am referring to. She took care of all of her kids. Christmas 96' was full of laughter, singing, jokes, horse playing, and lots and lots of delicious food, especially the gumbo. My grandmother made the best gumbo in the country, she was from New Orleans, Louisiana, and yes she even made it with okra (there's a lot of haters on okra being put into gumbo, but I love it). My aunts and their partners were there along with all my cousins. It was magical. To top things off, we all got a lot of presents (well, I know I did).

We had a pretty huge backyard, so the younger crowd played in the backyard with the new toys. Do you remember the safe sanctuary space you and your family built? For me and my cousins, it was our backyards. We loved playing freeze tag and hide-n-seek. We had this laundry pole that we would try to do our gymnastic flips on. Our grandparents loved the Olympics. They watched it often. We watched it often with them. Our whole family grew a love for sports. I will never forget the gymnastics team of 96, the magnificent seven (#DominiqueDawes).

This particular Christmas was one for the books. One with my grandmother and grandfather that my family will never forget. We all opened our gifts and took lots of pictures. There was a sense of love that filled the room with laughter and the true meaning of "Christmas" spirit abided.

That Christmas I got a little black puppy, a big wheel and some clothes as gifts. The same day that I got my puppy, I named him "Blacky." I guess it was my ignorance of not knowing how to feed a dog that led me to feeding him Chinese food. Oops. As a result, he died the next day. I felt devastated. I was young and dumb and did not know that Chinese food could kill dogs. That is the last thing I fed him before he died. It's possible something or someone else killed him. Whatever the truth may be, I have come to accept the conclusion that I killed my first dog.

That Christmas in particular, I thought I was cool. I was the gift wrapper. I loved helping mama with everything. They say to this today that I was the favorite. Again, I disagree. I thought my cousin, Anthony, held this trophy. Anthony was the oldest of the cousins in our generation. It was Anthony, Little Rick, Deon, Dionna, Myesha, Me, Lamar, CJ, John, and Domonique. My aunt had Anthony at an early age, so he was well taken care by my grandmother. It seemed like he could get away with anything. My grandmother gave him extra love in my eyes. He was smart, he played all the sports and he was respectful in listening and obeying the rules of the house. To top it all off, he always looked out for us growing up.

Even though this is true about Anthony, everyone says I was the favorite. As a result, I found myself inherently becoming mischievous and taking advantage of that position. My ego was building. My sense of doing as I pleased began to rise. I could do no evil. I could say no lie. And at times, I did some bad things. I even began to steal and lie.

I remember telling my grandfather that my brother was in the refrigerator eating and stealing some turkey. Our family was on a fixed income, so we could not just raid the refrigerator at will. There was breakfast, lunch and dinner. So, I lied on my brother Deon, and he got the best butt "whooping" of his life. CPS type beating. Because of things like this and other unknown reasons, my brother and I have an interesting relationship. He blames me for stuff I had no control over. Maybe that is why he still doesn't respect me. If this is the case, we should be even by now. He got his payback when he had this girl named Marcie, at our church in Fresno, beat me up. Yes, you read correctly. She beat me up in the church house! I mean she was older and I was always taught to never hit a lady. So, I let her win. I was always the smart one. Needless to say, I was so pissed at my brother.

Being raised in Fresno, allowed us to get a firm foundation. This was the first time I saw myself grow cognitively, mentally and spiritually. Fresno Temple Church of God in Christ under Bishop Wilson was the church we attended. Everything I am today, is because of this church. It brings back so many memories and my love for church began to flourish there. I had the best Sunday school teacher, Sis. Hall; and YPWW teachers, Melissa and Alicia. All of my mother's friends were there. And There I had the best choir directors and the best vacation bible school experiences.

We lived in Fresno from the time I was 4 until 12 years old. I loved to go to church. Every day when we were on break, I would make it my mission to go to noon day prayer with my grandmother. She was a praying mother, something that was passed down to me. She always encouraged me to pray, to trust God and to do well in school.

My other love besides church was school. I will never forget my first day of Kindergarten; my aunt Kelly took me to school at Lane

Elementary. She was more excited than I was. She told me if I have any problems, to come back and tell her. That day she instilled a level of confidence in me that still lingers today.

Kindergarten through second grade I thought the work was too easy. My cousin Myesha, who was two years older than me, would come over and teach me everything she learned and helped me with my homework. Cousins can play a critical and helpful role in someone's life. I was in "GATE" classes from 3rd grade until 6th grade. I was always a smart kid, but also a class clown. Because of this I would often find myself missing a lot of recesses. I would have to stand on the pole or sit in the classroom. I honestly think this was a form of torture. I remember one time I spread cherry juice all over my fifth grade teacher's door because I did not like her teaching style and honestly I thought she was mean towards me. I did get caught.

During this time, I was thought of as being a mean kid. I was far from being mean. I was just angry. Angry with myself because my parents were not there. Angry with my family because they never talked about my parents. Angry with God because here I was, a young boy with no parents to appreciate me as their own.

From there, I transferred to Baird Middle School. It was a school for the "gifted" and "talented" (but are standardized testing really true predictors of one's abilities?); it was called a "magnet" school. We had to test to get into the school, so when I got accepted, I was so proud. I remember dancing in the living room with my grandmother, while she laughed and smiled. At Baird, I cultivated a love for sports, I joined the volleyball team and the track team. One particular track meet I realized hurdles were not the event for me. I ran up to the very first hurdle and fell, so I stayed there. From that experience, I've realized in life there will be hurdles and it's up to us to either continue the race or stay there like I did on that day.

Unlike on that day, I couldn't just stay down when I experienced hurdles in life. This was mainly because of the black women in my life playing a vital role in more ways than one. They played an instrumental role in the successes of my life. My grandmother and aunts, Tracey, Kelly Gina, and all my girl cousins gave me a deeper appreciation for Black women. Each one had their own story. Yet, they were tough, resilient, vocal, loving, forgiving and fighters. Because of this, I had to be these things too.

Aunt Gina had some major mental health problems, but in the family, she was the best chef out of all my aunts. She was the "cook" after grandma. She made the best tacos. Even though she battled with having issues and mental health conditions, my aunt Gina is thriving as a nurse in the greater Los Angeles area, married to her partner, living in Lancaster, California, for over 10 years with a lot of beautiful grandkids. Everyone has to go through something before purpose takes a positive position.

Aunt Tracey, I have always considered her the smart one. She did everything she could do to do better for herself and her family. She was the giver. She had enlisted into the service, got married and had my favorite cousin, Myesha. Tracey retired at 50, doing major work in the justice system and even now has become actively involved in her community in Houston, Texas.

Aunt Kelly, I will always have a deep appreciation for my aunt Kelly. Mainly because she was a "gangsta" in her own right. In the family she is known as the "fighter." Her stories are so great that she will need to write her own book one day. My aunt Kelly survived the stigma and stress of giving birth as a young teenager. Can you imagine the pressure experienced during the 1980's as a young Black female in Los Angeles, California, in the hood? She is a true fighter for becoming the phenomenal woman she is today. My aunt Kelly is living in Fresno, California, happily with her husband.

Fresno was a place I called home. I hated that we had to move. But my aunt Tracey always looked out for everyone and called for us to move

33

down to Lancaster. She had gotten a phat job in Lancaster working in the Corrections Department. So she ended up buying our parents a house in Lancaster, CA. Apparently, my parents had been ready to leave because they willingly left.

Our move to Lancaster was for the good. Lancaster was amazing. Even though I had a positive support system around me in Lancaster, I didn't utilize it. I was always a sneaky and malicious kid. Mainly, because I felt I didn't have an outlet to discuss my issues. I remember there were two white kids down the street that were mean to my cousins and I. So, in return one day, I went to their backyard gate and let their dogs out. They never found them. I did get in huge trouble for this. But that didn't stop me. After this incident, I threw an orange through my neighbor's front window because I thought he was weird and I was ignorant of other cultures.

Unfortunately, my ignorance didn't stop there. As a confused young man, I would "borrow." It was a sport to me. I would "borrow" candy from my teacher's candy jars and money from classmates. I "borrowed" a lot too. Mainly because we were not pushed into doing sports, so we had a lot of extra time on our hands. And I chose to use my time doing juvenile things. Even though doing juvenile things was exhilarating and fun, on the inside, I ultimately knew it was wrong. I was just screaming and asking for help.

The sad reality was that at that time, no one would ever think it was me doing all those mischievous things because I was labeled as a "good" kid. But I was crying out for attention. I was desperate for attention. I needed someone, anyone to talk to. But I felt like I had no one.

Now that I look back, I think the need to have someone to talk to wasn't just my need. But it's the need of a lot of young people. I think that the Black Family doesn't spend enough time talking to their children. The reality is that we like to hide things. We share what we want especially if there isn't a consistent outlet. I know that I did this a lot as a teenager. As a result, I had a variety of passions, some good and some bad. So much so, that I began to freely cultivate a new passion of mine, pornography.

Pornography was interesting, exhilarating and intriguing. Our family never had the conversation about sex, but porn allowed me to experience "sex" through a different lens. I learned about breasts, penises, anal and much more through this television experience. I learned about the concept of masturbation through this, too. It resulted in me having fantasies with both women and men. I found myself placing myself in sexual fantasies. Which I soon would act out in my adult life.

Now Let's Uncover memories

Childhood Memories: Everyone has them, but when is the last time you thought about them? What was some of your favorite childhood memories?

Who were in the memories? Friends? Family?

_____
_____
_____
_____
_____

What feeling(s) were produced by these memories?

_____
_____
_____
_____
_____
_____
_____
_____
_____
_____
_____

What are you going to do with these memories?

_____
_____
_____
_____
_____

Hold fast to your favorite memories.

CHAPTER 4:

LANCASTER, CA

————◆————

For I know the thoughts that I think toward you, saith the LORD,
thoughts of peace, and not of evil, to give you an expected end. - Jeremiah
29:11

According to kidsdata.org, 7.5% of Los Angeles County population are of
the foster youth demographic.

"Y̶ou were so young when it happened!" My sister Kim told
me. I lost my mom, my grandmother, Geraldine Cromwell,
that raised me from two days old until I was 15 years old. I
was in the 10th grade. The date was October 26, 2001. We got the call
from my grandfather. He and my aunt had been at the hospital. They
called to tell us she left us. You could hear the anguish and sadness in
my grandfather's voice. My aunt Tracey said, "She didn't want to be
caught up in tubes. That wasn't my mother." My mom, Geraldine, was
a fighter, a lover, a giver, a helper, a spiritual woman of God who
dedicated herself to her family. Even though we did not have the same
blood, she raised me as her own… and I was her family too.

The father on my birth certificate, Gerald Green, was her son, but my
birth mother, Denise Carter, whom I never met, wasn't the child of
Geraldine. My aunt had gotten the call saying "if you want him, come
get him NOW!" Unaware of what I was to become, she kept me. Even
despite her husband voting against it. My grandfather, Herbert

Cromwell, was a proud man. He was a strong, fun and compassionate individual. He was a tall 6'2 Black veteran of the United States Army and had four kids. Two with my grandmother and two with another woman. My aunt Tracey told me on my "home alone" Christmas trip "my father (Herbert) was tired, and he did not think he was going to keep you for a long time." I think the reason he voted against me was because he was tired of raising kids. But my grandmother understood the power of a support system. To make matters even more difficult, there was a huge gap in age. He was 54 years older than me. So, imagine gaining another child in your 50s and 60s. I would have been tired too.

Despite the age difference and the lack of energy, my grandparents still decided to raise me as their own. This is something that society must give honor to. Regardless of the dysfunctions, trauma and horrid backgrounds Black families have had, they did whatever had to be done for the family to survive. There seems to be an unspoken mandate that you must take care of everyone and not really enjoy life like our white counterparts do. The Black grandparent is so instrumental and monumental in the family structure that if they did not provide for their grandchildren, a lot of their grandchildren would end up dead, in jail, in the psych ward or in the foster care system.

Keeping the family together and safe wasn't the only thing grandparents did, they also kept their secrets from their children and other loved ones. I believe it is an unspoken rule of the older generations to not share everything with everybody. Secrets that could help those like me, understand a little more of who they are, should not remain hidden forever. And honestly, because of this, I have some regrets. I regret not being able to dig or ask questions regarding my grandfather and mom's (grandmother) life.

Geraldine and Herbert Cromwell were good at keeping secrets. Even though they were not my secrets, they were the worst kind. I did not know my biological mother was a prostitute. She sold her body for money. I did not know my father was a "john," that no one would ever know anything about. I did not know that my "mother" was not my blood. Secrets have an impact not only on the ones holding them, but on those they are held to protect. Because of this withholding of secrets by my parents, I did not know my brother Deon and I had different dads. It wasn't until I got older and after my grandparents passed away that that secret was revealed to me through aunts and uncles.

Despite the secrets that were kept, my grandparents consistently took care of me as if those secrets did not exist. We moved to Lancaster, CA in 1998. I was heading into my seventh year and I did not know what to expect. We just moved to a better neighborhood, so I thought. I made some new cool friends. I started junior high school at New Vista Middle School. It was there my love for volleyball and track was cultivated. We started attending Faith Chapel North COGIC, under Pastor Darryl Jackson. Although, I hated that we moved away from Fresno, I got used to it; I began to love it. I was a smart kid, so I thought.

New Vista Middle School was pretty dope. Despite having to wear uniforms, I made friends pretty easy. Despite what people think of me today, then, I was shy. I was intimidated. I had more feminine tendencies than most males. I liked to run and play volleyball, and according to gender roles, that is a "woman's" sport. I mean, in 4th grade I was a cheerleader. Yes, I know, a cheerleader. More so, yell squad. Anyways, I joined the volleyball and track team and I excelled. In 8th grade, we won the championship against Hill View. That was a day I will never forget because that was our toughest game. But it wasn't the toughest for me, at least mentally.

Antelope Valley High School would be my next tough adventure. Four years of self-discovery. Maturing into a young man with no true male guidance. Yes, my grandfather was there, however, because of the significant age gap, there was only so much he could do. I lost my grandmother sophomore year. I was lost and in full confusion. So, I was taken under the ministerial staff at the church. I became a licensed minister at the age of 15 in the Pentecostal denomination Church of God In Christ (C.O.G.I.C.), I knew God had a plan for my life despite my addiction to porn and desire to like men.

I loved watching porn. It started in Fresno, when we had the "black box." You know the one where the illegal cable and nasty channels (pornography) was free. During this time, I would sneak into the room and watch it from the outside. But now in Lancaster, my cousin had porn magazines and videos hidden. Which I found, watched and fantasized about.

Aside from watching pornography on the television, or looking at the naked bodies in magazines, I ventured to the internet. At that time, the internet was on a porn rise. I would watch it when I was at my aunt's, supposedly working on my homework. I was hooked to the point that I watched porn at school. One day I even got caught looking at porn in my 9th grade class. It was so embarrassing. But it didn't stop me because I was both intrigued and curious.

Me being curious did not start with me watching porn either. Growing up, I had always been a curious person (which I think adds value to my personality). However, I was also too grown for my own good. Unfortunately, this had disastrous consequences for me. At 15, I was molested by an older guy at the gym. That would be my first "gay" experience as the church and society would say.

The life altering incident took place early one morning, 3:00 am to be exact. I remember it vividly. That morning I backed my grandmother's car out of the garage. To do this, I manually lifted up the garage door, put the car in neutral, pushed the car back and when it rolled down, I would run fast, hop in, park the car, let down the garage door and then start it outside where no one could hear the engine start. Sounds like a lot, right? It was!

After successfully backing the car out silently, I drove to 24 hour fitness to workout. I had gotten free guest passes from one of the school's basketball players. So, I went there to workout, not sure of what I was doing. From across the room, this guy kept walking by and looking, but I didn't know what to expect. So, I minded my own business and continued to work out. After the workout, I went to shower and the 6'1 bi-racial buff guy kept walking by and looking (just an FYI, this happens still today in gyms all over the country). I felt like I was in a porn. Images from past pornography kept going through my mind. After that, I went to the sauna and then he came in, naked. I was unsure of what to do and how to get out of this predicament. He kept getting closer and closer and told me I needed to give in. So, I did what he asked. I gave in.

After that experience, I felt ashamed and weird with this new secret. I had always imagined that it would happen, but I was not sure of when and with who. This man was 20 plus years older than me. I later found out he was a security guard for the local high school. He not only violated me, but other students across the Antelope Valley. I had always thought I was the one wrong for doing it because I had thought it in my head.

But the reality is that this old man knew better.
He should have done better.

The sad reality is older males are out there preying on the young every day. This is something that is pervasive in the church. Older men prey. Bishops, Elders and Ministers try to hide their desire for men but behind closed doors are raping and taking young boys mind and body. I mean look at the Pope and the Catholic church. This is universal! They prey on these younger boys and girls, wanting to take their innocence. It is our job as community stakeholders to protect our youth and young adults. I do believe that these people can be forgiven, people can be healed but that is through their testimony and repentance. To take someone's innocence with no knowledge of the whole situation, is absolutely disgusting.

Growing up, I knew that I liked men and wanted to try it out, and some wanted to try me too. At the age of 12 years old, I found myself having crushes on and desiring famous celebrities on television. It made me feel different. I felt like I could not talk about it because in church this "sin" is like the absolute *worst* sin. This is what has been preached about and condemned over the pulpit for years. However, the bible says the one that sows discord is an abomination too (Proverbs 6:16-19) but that would be rarely preached over the pulpit, because church people are messy.

I was called out over the pulpit when I was 17 years old. I remember being at a revival service, and the guest preacher called me "out" in front of the entire church. He said, "you are dealing with some heavy spirits, one in particular is a homosexual spirit." I did not know what to do. I was in shock. I was low-key embarrassed. But I got prayed for and thought it would go away. I felt good for the moment after they prayed for me too. I was confident that the "homosexual" spirit would go away. But it didn't. I ultimately felt ashamed, embarrassed and angry with the preacher for doing that. It was none of anyone's business what I was dealing with, so I thought.

I remember on the drive home with my foster brother Darrell, he asked me "did you always know?" I said "yes." He did not know how to handle it. Even though this was the case we talked about it. He said, "we thought maybe you were dealing with it, especially Pumpkin, but we didn't know how to talk to you about it."

I believe they didn't know how to talk about it because they saw the call on my life. They saw how God used me. Even though it's unbelievable, it still didn't take away from who God called me to be. A call that I accepted at a very young age. I remember that day clearly. I walked by my pastor, Darryl Jackson's, office and told him "I think the Lord is calling me to preach!" He said, "Good! Get a sermon ready for next week!" So, I did.

At the age of 14, I gave my first message at my church, Faith Chapel North COGIC; it was on Colossians 3:5 - and let the peace of God rule in your hearts. My grandmother was there when I preached. I remember her smiling and being super proud of me. It is something that I miss: being in her presence. I ministered to them about God's peace is the faith that would take us through our trials and tribulations. The hard reality is that we deal with so much mentally, physically, spiritually, and not just as Christians, but as human beings. Often times, because of what we deal with, we tend to lose sight of the bigger picture. We lose hope. We doubt God. We doubt ourselves.

Reflecting back on it now, I realize a lot about peace and how it applies to my life. Peace is so hard to come around to as a Black male in a white society. It was hard for me to navigate my peace at UCLA too. We must remember that the Black experience is not monolithic. I was bi-racial, light skinned so some of my trials were different. Some Black people don't know or will never know what true peace is. We have to work tirelessly to pay the bills, while taking care of our and others children, to make ends meet. We have to help all of our families out when hard times come. We have to worry about police killing our loved ones. We have to worry about "if I am going to get pulled over today?" We have to figure out will our mouth and body be policed and subjected to harassment and violence. Blackness is a threat to society. But it is because of one's perception gained through media and representations in our books and on the television. Black people have to live in a fear of danger on a daily basis…. Have you ever felt like this?

Often times, for Black people there is no safe space for this nostalgic peace.

The sense of peace I had gained from preaching that sermon quickly became tested. After losing my grandmother, I ended up moving into my aunt Tracey's house. I enjoyed my time there, but the troubles of my past followed me. I had no respect for myself. This lack of respect spilled over and resulted in me not having any respect for others.

My lack of respect for others led to me taking things without permission. On my second day of my senior year, I borrowed my cousin's car to get a pair of shoes from my friend's house in Palmdale. As I was traveling there, the phone fell underneath the steering wheel. I reached down to get it. When I got up from getting the phone, next thing I heard was POW! I crashed into the back of a truck that had no brake lights. I temporarily lost consciousness. I woke up facing the opposite way in a totaled car.

When my aunt went to the junkyard, they told her that they didn't know how I made it out. From there it went downhill. I had to go to jail. My aunt actually pressed charges on me. As a result, I had to do community service. Anger, confusion and sadness were feelings that I felt towards my aunt. I was young and dumb and did not know how to handle my emotions. We were not taught how to handle our emotions growing up. We were always taught to obey and do not talk back. I can't blame my aunt for reacting the way she did, I would have done the same. She was not my biological mother, so what more could she have done. She always tried to help out everyone in the family. But you can only help so many people for only so long. You can't help people that don't want help.

As a result of my immaturity and feelings, I ended up running away and leaving my aunt's. I felt she gave up on me. So, I did the only thing I knew to resolve the situation. I left.

From there I ended up going to a group home in Chatsworth, right across from the Northridge mall. In the van ride heading to the group home, I was unsure of what to expect. I was in a confused state of mind. I was angry at my family. And sad that my mother wasn't there to protect me. (Have you ever felt like your loved ones have given up on you?).

The month that I was there waiting to get adopted, was like hell! It was like jail. We had to wake up and go to bed at a certain time. There was a lock on the refrigerator.
I was not used to this.
There was a gate around the pool with a lock.
I was not used to this.
I could only make phone calls on the weekend.
I was not used to this.
I had no visitors. And besides that,
I had to share a room with 4 other guys.
I was not used to this, too.

I had no time for myself. There were mandatory hours of doing homework. We had two hours on the weekend to go to the mall and do something. It was a horrible experience. I felt bad for the other guys there because they did not have any family to reach out to. This is something that is drastically over looked in Black and Brown communities. As horrible as my experience was, this is where I developed a desire to own a chain of group homes. This is where I gained a sense of how our foster care systems in America and in California are pervasive and how important the role of placement and advocacy for foster youths is critical and necessary.

After being there for a month, I moved in with my foster family, the Dorris family. Besides my grandmother being the most influential person in my life, there was Darrell and Roshunda Dorris. Roshunda and Darrell both knew my grandmother, so it was like getting adopted back into my family.

They stepped up to the plate when all my other family did not know what to do. They both understood that everyone comes from different backgrounds. They understood that no one is perfect. This understanding came from love! It is love that everyone needs and desires, so it does not make sense to condemn or judge the next person.

Because of them, mom Verniette Dorris accepted me and decided to take me in. As a result, I gained three more brothers, Darrell, Marcus and Lee. And one foster sister, Brigette. They understood the complexity of my childhood, but still loved on me.

I had to gain thick skin around them. I was used to being around women growing up, so now with brothers constantly cracking jokes and playing around, I couldn't be as timid or as shy. I have always been an outspoken person, but becoming a part of this family required me to be even more outspoken.

Being around them was a blessing. I found a new love for church, life and the idea of what a true family consisted of. Darrell and Roshunda knew me from when I was at Faith Chapel North, when my grandmother was still alive. I consider them to be the two realest and empowering people I know. Darrell is a jokester that loves to laugh, but also is about his business and family. Roshunda is more of the quiet one, but very nurturing and strategic in her delivery. So, thankfully, there was a level of understanding between us.

They were my youth pastors. And I must say we had one of the best youth departments in Lancaster. I think it was Darrell's candid personality that drew me to them. He went out of his way to become my mentor. Before my grandmother left, he took on that role. We would go downtown and buy suits, and go to concerts and host events that helped to nurture my faith in God.

Darrell wasn't the only one who helped to nurture me, mom Dorris did as well. I remember going into her house behind 30 units. This forced me to go into independent study. I had to stop going to the normal schooling period and isolate myself at an off-campus classroom. This was the best decision at the time. I worked hard. She encouraged me every day on the way to school. She would say, "Chris, you can do this! Do not quit." These encouraging words are what I hold dear today.

At that time, I would always ask myself whether I would have been able to accomplish what I was able to accomplish had my mom been alive. I accomplished so much during a small period of time. I worked hard completing one packet at a time each week. Sometimes, I even turned in three to four packets a week with each packet gaining one credit. Because I worked so hard, I finished a month earlier than expected. The feeling of reward was something that no one could take away from me. No one could take away from the things I had accomplished!

After my big accomplishment, I got my first job at good ol' McDonald's. I ended up working at two McDonald's. I worked at one the summer before for two months until I got fired. I ended up getting fired because I said something I should not have said. Something I will not repeat in this book.

After being fired from that McDonald's, I was fortunate enough to get hired working at another location. At this second location, I worked with my brother, Lee, who just happened to be the manager.

Working at McDonalds with my older brother Lee was interesting and fun. I absolutely loved our time together. I learned my lesson from the other McDonald's. This time, I was careful to watch what I said and to whom I said it to. I now knew and understood that you cannot trust everyone. And that you cannot believe that everyone will hold you down or keep your secrets.

At the second Mc Donald's location, I got to work full time. I liked working the register and the driveway. However, sometimes there were discrepancies with hyper specific customers that truly wanted everything their way. I will never forget working the front register and a customer came in and asked for the manager. She told her, "I did not want mustard on this burger!" and threw the burger into the manager's face. If you know anything about me, I have a problem with holding my laughter. I ran into the back and laughed so hard. What else could I do?

I worked at this McDonalds for eight months until I moved out of my foster mom's house. I had to move out because I was facing serious issues with my sexuality. I find that a lot of people do not like to talk about struggling with one's sexuality because of the fear of judgement from people. I've come to realize that more people need to talk about this struggle. While on the flip side, other people need to mind their own business if they don't know anything about this struggle. Both sides of my families knew about my sexual identity issues. Despite that, both sides of my family have always loved on me. One side didn't condone it, and the other did not care.

Because of this, I decided I had to go out and try it for myself. While I was working at McDonalds, I found out about this phone chat room called "the party line." It was notorious for hookups for both men and women. I met a guy, as well as others, off the chatroom at McDonalds. I never did hook up with this guy. However, he was the doorway to going to this club called the "Arena" every Wednesday night in Hollywood.

My foster mom and brother went to sleep the same time every night. I used their routine to my advantage to sneak out of the house undetected. To get back in undetected, I would leave the door unlocked. Because of the ease, sneaking out of the house became frequent.

We would leave around 10:30 pm every night to drive down to Hollywood. We would party and then sneak back in. This occurred until I finally got caught. My foster mom said "you will have to decide what you want to do, but it is not allowed under this roof"

Although I got caught, I couldn't stop. The door had been opened. The chatroom was the pathway to my wilderness. Even though this was the case, I am thankful for all of the doors that were opened and closed during this season and every other season. Why? Because I've learned that everything that happens in our lives happens for a reason. The reason is to add value and worth to our lives!

Let's Uncover your doors

Can you identify times in your life where one decision sent you to a door that led you down a path you considered, but hadn't thought of? What was it?

_____

_____

_____

_____

_____

_____

_____

_____

_____

_____

_____

_____

_____

_____

_____

What did you do to recover?

_____

_____

_____

_____

_____

_____

_____

_____

_____

_____

_____

If you have yet to recover, what do you think you can do to recover?

The doors we open can catapult us in a positive or negative direction. No matter what direction you go, YOU have what it takes to recover.

CHAPTER 5:

MY WILDERNESS AND TRANSITION THE VALLEY
(Chatsworth, Northridge, NoHo and Houston, TX)

———◆———

Yea, though I walk through the valley of the shadow of death, I will fear no evil: for thou art with me; thy rod and thy staff they comfort me. - Psalms 23:4

According to kidsdata.org, 22% of Texans foster youth are African Americans.

My foster mom said, "either you are going to abide by my rules or leave," so me being me, I said yes. Yes, I will leave, and there I went. I left the key on the counter and moved. Unsure of where to go, but I had an idea. For the last two months of the summer of 2004, I had been sneaking in and out of the house driving back and forth to Hollywood to go to a club called the Arena. It was an 18 and over club and it was lit. It was primarily Black folk and people of color. The music was banging. The friends I met while working at McDonalds introduced me to this club and to my new lifestyle. My new best friend, Terrell, let me stay with him and his family until I could go elsewhere. I left the church. I left my foster family. I left what I thought I needed to leave behind. Even though I left them, I would soon find out that family is what I needed the most.

I moved from house to house, couch to couch, until I finally found an apartment for foster youth through the Penny Lane Center. My roommate was also a foster youth; he had this crazy eye, that my friends made fun of him for. I didn't join in because I felt a sense of compassion for him. This compassion for him would quickly decrease once I discovered he was also a thief. He stole a lot of money from me. I had put the money away because I did not trust our banking system (and still don't today). I was 18 and I knew nothing about transitioning into adulthood, but I thought I was grown. After the encounter with the thief, I was kicked out of the program because of physical altercations.

After being kicked out, I met some friends from Lancaster, California, that took me on a journey that was unexpected. We would travel together. We traveled from New York, Houston, New Orleans, Atlanta, Chicago and the Bay Area. We would steal clothes and food together. We would get into fights together. It was a lot. I wanted to fit in. I wanted to impress people so much that I did things that made some not like me. I was lost.

During this time, I was submerged in a wilderness period to say the least. I was living from house to house. And when there wasn't a house as an option, I lived from hotel to hotel. I couldn't get a stable place of my own because I had no established credit. And I was too prideful to call my family for help. I felt I was doing the right thing, but was alone… or at least I felt like it.

One drunken night after the club, I met my first partner, Deavine, who is still one of my close friends. He stayed at CSUN and we lived as best as we could in a college dormitory. The dorm Deavine lived in, was a studio. The apartment still had hall monitors whose assignments were to monitor the residents just like in a regular dorm. Because Deavine's friend was the monitor, we never faced issues with me living there. We never got caught.

At 18 and 19, I thought I was living the life. Going to fashion shows, balls, shopping sprees, clubs, drinking, smoking weed and traveling. However, we had our negative moments.

I got caught stealing from Macy's. We were headed to Atlanta, Georgia for this huge event and I needed clothes. I ultimately got charged with a misdemeanor and had to do community service; even though this was over 13 years ago, I am still denied jobs because of it today. I finally was able to get it expunged in 2018. But for some jobs I still have to disclose it, which I find to be contradictory. It is crazy how people just don't understand how our criminal justice system works or not work. It is inconsiderate of people's position in life.

After the arrest, we had to move because my partner ended up leaving school. We moved into an amazing apartment near the Sherman Oaks Galleria. Sherman Oaks was an area that was more than what I was used too. Prior to moving there, I experienced a nice life growing up in houses, not apartments. But this place was my own. It was built like a resort. It had palm trees. It had a huge pool. And the overall environment was cool. I loved this place so much that I would host various gatherings to show it off. Life was great in the Oaks. . . or so I thought.

One day, on my way to show my best friend my apartment, we got pulled over. I was driving with no license and I was taken to jail, yes again. Thankfully this encounter with jail was just a warning. However, it was soon followed by another.

We moved from Sherman Oaks to North Hollywood where I got caught up with some bad friends. These bad connections lead to my "wilderness" moment at Twin Towers. I had warrants for not showing up to court and not completing my community service. I was arrested in Palmdale and was transferred from the Lancaster jail to Palmdale court to handle my case. I plead guilty and had to serve 30 days. I thought I was going to die.

After being handed my "death sentence," we got on the bus to Twin Towers. To my surprise, I already knew a couple of people who I thought would have my back. I was instantly relieved

This moment of relief was short-lived as soon as I met with the psychologist. The psychologist based whether or not to put me in regular population on one question: "why don't you want to go up there?" And I said, "I think they are gonna kill me!"

Now look y'all, I was 19, young, still unsure of my sexuality and identity, and I was afraid. My parents would always watch criminal justice shows, especially Law and Order. As a result of what I saw, I knew that jail was not the place for me. Even though I was born in a jail cell, both of my families tried to protect me from it. I saw stories on television of men being raped and heard stories from family members, and I just knew that was not the place I needed to be.

As a result of me admitting that I thought they were going to kill me, they put me in the mental ward. Yes, the psych ward. SMH. My next cell neighbor, someone that deserved to be there, would scream crazy things all day and beat on the toilet most of the day. And to make things even worse, I didn't even have a blanket to sleep under... My blanket was literally a strait jacket.

There was no sense of humanity in that place. Fortunately for me I was released earlier than expected. After being in hell on earth for 14 days I was released back into civilization. Upon release the psychologist said, "you didn't deserve to be here!" To which I replied, "I have been saying this the whole time!"

Although my stay in jail was only 14 days, it felt like forever. To be caged up in a cell and not being able to leave, frightened me! I couldn't understand, and still don't understand, how people are not scared but love going back. Aside from feeling caged, I was ashamed, scared, angry, sad, and disappointed! I literally cried myself to sleep every night.

During my jail stay, my emotions were exacerbated because Deavine wasn't there. Although we were arrested together, he didn't have to endure what I endured. His parents bailed him out. Because my family did not know too much about my situation, they really couldn't help me. I could not call them and beg for them to come help me. I had to learn the "hard way."

As difficult as the experience of going to jail was, it was the best thing for me. There is where my mindset changed. I decided then that that had to be my last time going... My worth was more than being in the place where I had been born: a jail cell.

From there I went on a journey of trying to survive. I ended up going into male sex work. It was a generational curse that I never paid attention to. I loved sex, so why not get paid for it? I knew it was wrong and a lessening of my values, but what better way was there to live a life of fast money. I wanted to be fabulous. I wanted money. I wanted the best. And even while writing this I had to pray that people reading this does not turn up their nose at my choice of living. I had to survive. But while doing it, I traveled all over the country meeting new people and making money. Nonetheless, still there was a void.

One night while in a hotel with my friends E and G listening to a gospel classic, "Endow Me," something happened, something broke. It was in that moment that the song ministered to me. I knew that my grandmother and God wanted more for me. It was in that moment I kept hearing my grandmother's voice saying, "you are better than this." It was in that moment that I decided I had to change. Something had to change.

After that night, I moved to Houston Texas for six months, expecting change. But even there, I wasn't able to escape the generational curses of drugs, alcohol and sex. I knew it was because of my surroundings. I do believe that you must surround yourselves with people that you want to be like. But one of my philosophies at the time was to always try something, and if I did not like it, then to stop it. Because of this, I was taking drugs every week. We traveled from Houston to New Orleans, to D.C., to New York, to Phoenix and other cities to make money for rent and other expenses.

At the time I thought I was living a real good life. But in actuality I lost sight of my true value. I knew something had to change. So, one day, I packed my bags and returned back to California in hopes of doing something different. I was able to make this move because of the experience I gained as a foster youth… the experience of picking up and leaving at a drop of a dime.

When I returned to California, I had to get a job, but it was hard. So, I continued sex work on the side, but I did not indulge as much. During this time, I moved into a household with a couple. He and his partner worked for the state of California, but still opened their doors to me. I was very appreciative of them. But I still felt something was missing. Although I was living in Lancaster, I remained cut off from both sides of my family.

This wilderness part of my life was something I refused to share with my family and friends. Even while I write and include this in my book, I am asking myself if this is too much to share??? But as I have grown over time, I've arrived at the conclusion that there is no such thing as being too real. We all must be truthful with our reality. Facing our reality and our experiences are what keeps us sane and determined to not give up on our faith in God. We all have our own journeys, but it is our process that helps us develop our purpose.

I've come to realize over my thirty-two years of living that people will talk about you regardless. They will question you. They will attack you. I think it is because they do not understand or agree with the choices we have made. But have they paid any of your bills? Or tried to help you? I believe in telling the truth because there was a time in my life when I would lie just for fun. Now that I have grown and matured, I've come to realize that there is no need to lie or hide anything.

The church has taught us while growing up that "everyone doesn't need to know your business," but my question or critique of this is, why not? Why can't I share my experiences? Isn't this supposed to help others get through their hardships? Their doubts? Their insecurities? We all have secrets, but I believe God wants us to move out of this phase of hiding to digging deep and uncover our worth.

Today's generation is facing suicide because they feel as if no one understands them, when there are some that do. Our ancestors did not pave the way by sacrificing their lives for us to not have a safe zone or space. I understand this all too well. I have thought about killing myself. Honestly, suicidal thoughts played often in my mind after my grandmother's passing. I felt like I had lost everything. I felt like why should I live? Why did God allow this to happen? What was His reasoning for putting me out on my own? Why should I exist? What value did my life have if there were no one around? But it is nothing but by God's grace and my faith that I have continued to push toward understanding my worth and value. All so I can try and help others see their value and worth.

It takes time…. And transparency.

Now Let's Uncover your wilderness
What did or does your wilderness look like?

_____
_____
_____
_____
_____
_____
_____
_____
_____
_____
_____
_____
_____
_____
_____
_____

How has this experience shaped you?

_____
_____
_____
_____
_____
_____
_____
_____

What will you share with others to help them?

The wilderness will open your eyes! We all have a wilderness. It will push you to doing better and becoming the best person you can be.

PART II

CHAPTER 6:

SACRAMENTO, CA

"And the son said unto him, Father, I have sinned against heaven, and in thy sight, and am no more worthy to be called thy son. But the father said to his servants, Bring forth the best robe, and put it on him; and put a ring on his hand, and shoes on his feet" - Luke 15: 21, 22

According to kidsdata.org, 23.7% of the foster youth demographic are African Americans

I was a country boy, because of my grandmother and grandfather, living in small rural areas. I was sheltered growing up. Because of this, moving to Los Angeles, and living in the valley became too much for me. So, I relocated up north to Sacramento as previously mentioned to live with my sister and her eight kids. While I was there, I furthered my education, my faith and my resume.

I decided to get back into church. I went to All Nations COGIC with my sister, Tameka. I joined the choir. I went to Bible Study every week. I was at church every Sunday. I had to pray and praise this "gay" away. It was not of God as I was told. I have always had a love for God and his Word, it's like I said earlier, I was a licensed minister at fifteen years of age. I got heavily involved into the ministry. I wanted to do right by God according to the bible as I had been taught since birth. I wanted to be "right."

In a quest to do right I started dating women again. The women I dated at the first church were very controlling but yet loving. However, even while dating them I was still being contacted by my old flings and would find myself in a battle.

So, I decided within myself that it was best for me to be open about my "struggle" with my sexuality. I told my pastor and the assistant pastor about my struggle with homosexuality. My transparency didn't go well.

I don't blame them anymore for the way they reacted. Mainly, because the leadership there was family operated, like most churches, which isn't necessarily a bad thing. But these environments usually foster the very heteronormative and conservative ideology that do not allow others to learn their gifts and operate according to God's will. Because of this, I felt like being gay was a problem in the church. It's what most preachers talk about and preach against. The sad reality is that some of the very ones preaching against it are sometimes homosexual themselves. Boom! *shrugs shoulders*

They told me, "you need to sit down from everything." I left the meeting offended but respected it. But when they told me I needed to sit down, all kinds of emotions emerged. I felt angry, disappointment, shame, guilt, sadness, confusion and fear. I knew God had plans for my life but here were two very patriarchal heteronormative men that told me otherwise. I could have sued them. I thought about going to the news on them but I knew I was bigger than that. They were purposely designed to add value to my life, and it did.

Even though they told me to sit down, I couldn't. I knew there was more to my calling than just sitting in a pew. Especially, when most of the men that are caught abusing young boys are of clergy. In fact, there had been a man that was charged with rape of a young woman but yet when I was honest, they threw me away. I was tired of being thrown away. I had been dealing with being given up on all my life. So, I left.

From that moment forward I saw church through a different lens as I got older. Sin became more visible. I saw the life of preachers hitting on young men, i.e. me. I would hold out as much as I could. If I "slipped," I prayed and fasted and kept reading the bible. I ended up going to another church, Blessed Faith. This church had more young adults and were up to my speed in regards to living in transparency.

The Bible simply demands us to love one another as he has loved the church. So, even if I was dealing with homosexuality, and someone was dealing with adultery, it is not the place of others to place their views or judgements on my life or anyone else's. God will deal with everything at the end of the day.

What I've come to realize is that people like to be in other people's business so that they can hold something over one's head. Bribery of exposure is a huge phenomenon in the church. I have always been upfront about my "thorn," and my "iniquities" with my leaders and family. But their love is what kept me wanting more of God. It's what fueled a desire for me to build my own personal relationship with God.

Although this is the case, typing this or telling this is still hard to do, because of the backlash this may cause. Nevertheless, I know I must tell it because the Word tells us we overcome by the words of our testimony and by the blood of Jesus (Rev 12:11). Therefore, I'm telling my testimony, because I overcame. And I continue to overcome!

I tell it also because I believe millennials are tired of religion and tradition. They are tired of the fake and phony. Reality is, some rules and regulations within the church are man-made and can do more harm than good. This is why it's important to have a relationship with God, so that people's opinions become less concerning and intimidating. Through this book, I want people to develop their own relationship with God and increase their own level of faith. The devil comes to steal, kill and destroy but it is God and the blood of Jesus that gives us life, liberty and the true pursuit of happiness.

I found happiness through God and the blood of Jesus. While working and going back to church full time, I found a love for God and his people. I started a young adult ministry with a couple of my fellow colleagues Dene and Paul. It was an amazing experience and lives were literally changed. We gave back to the homeless, we visited the sick and shut in, we mentored youth and I even started my own nonprofit called Church Geeks.

It was in this nonprofit I made it my endeavor to give back to those less fortunate even though I was not rich yet. The importance of giving back is something I learned from Geraldine and Darrell. They constantly stressed that "it is always better to give than it is to receive." As a result of this philosophy, we held services every other month at various churches. We made some cool t-shirts and fundraised through merchandise and was able to fund our activities and scholarships. We were fortunate to give away a book scholarship and some money. I understand that everyone is not blessed with the same opportunities or equal access to the same resources so it was my duty as a giver to give back. I worked faithfully and tirelessly but still for some this was not enough. I had always given and worked for other dreams but it was time for me to worry about mine.

After four and a half years of living in Sacramento, California, I decided to chase the dream God had given me while I lived in Lancaster. At that time I was only 16 years old. My other youth pastor, Pastor Richardson (who was another part of my support system) took us to UCLA. It was during that trip that I knew it! I knew I would be at UCLA. That day as I stood on UCLA's campus, I told myself "I am going to graduate from this place!"

Now Let's Uncover how your actions have impacted the next generation
This is something I want to challenge each one of you to do: think about the generations that will be coming after us.

What can we do to help push their dreams? And not just ours?

_____
_____
_____
_____
_____
_____
_____
_____
_____
_____
_____
_____
_____
_____

How can we make a difference in their lives?

_____
_____
_____
_____
_____
_____
_____
_____
_____
_____

Ask yourself, how can I help add value to their dreams and visions? How can I help them uncover their worth and purpose?

_____
_____
_____
_____
_____
_____
_____
_____
_____
_____
_____
_____
_____
_____

Your testimony is the key to someone else overcoming!

CHAPTER 7:

WALNUT, CA

———————◆———————

Trust in the Lord with all thine heart; and lean not unto thine own understanding. In all thy ways acknowledge him, and he shall direct thy paths. - Proverbs 3:5,6

According to kidsdata.org, 29.1% of the foster youth, are African American.

I prayed and fasted for three days before hearing God say "Trust me!" I knew it was time to leave after four and a half years in Sacramento, California. My philosophy was, if I can put almost five years into working I can definitely put the same amount of time into my education. It took a while to get all my options together and after that I was definitely leaning towards the transfer route. Was it going to be UC Davis? Or my dream school, UCLA? I had created a great family and semi-support system but I did not want to leave. This was a huge leap of faith, but I knew what vision I had and that was to attend UCLA! I knew this defining moment would indefinitely add worth to my story.

I relocated from Sacramento with a car full of belongings. I packed everything that could fit, and left to Claremont, California. Prior to leaving, I researched which community college would be the best route to get into UCLA. My friend, who taught, told me about the "Harvard" of community colleges- Mount San Antonio College in

Walnut California ("Mt. Sac"). Upon this advice, and conducting an ample amount of research I up and went. This was by far my best experience and I knew it was ordained by God.

There, at Mt. Sac, in Walnut, California I met Linda Diaz, whom I love dearly. The first day I met her, I asked "what do I need to do to get in at UCLA. I heard I can get there from here." Immediately, she pulled out my transcripts and went to work. Counselors, the right ones, who genuinely care about the student's aspirations, can play a huge critical empowering role in one's life. After looking them over she matched it with the IGETC (google this if you are interested in the transfer route) and there began my full time student journey.

I enrolled into an African American history class and a speech honors course. These two classes were on another level of critical thinking and required an ample amount of hard work. As a first semester full time student, it was something I had never experienced. Especially, my speech honors class. Fortunately for me I met my future fairy godparents, Liesel Reinhart and Kenny Klawitter in this class. Those two, with their rigorous, difficult and challenging speech classes, pushed me to pursue speech and debate also known as forensics.

I took their advice and joined the team. As a result, I met Sowmya, Barrett, Connie, Jon, Josh, Chidi, Anthony, Matt, Alejandra, Schaup, Kristen and Jendi. Together, we made up the Gold Winning MT SAC Forensics team for 2013-2014. Because of this experience, I strongly advocate for students to get involved in organizations and clubs on campuses. Aside from these great individuals there were other great friends I met on this journey. My coaches, Danny, Jeff, Kenny, Liesel and Roger. This was the start of the beginning of a new family and support system; to which I owe my success to.

I started off doing debate with Sowmya. After a while I didn't feel like reading a lot about current events. So, I moved over into the acting and theatrical side, called oral interpretation. I specifically loved poetry. My National Poetic Interpretation Gold winning piece was entitled: The Blerd (Black Nerd).

Even though my experience was amazing, I still felt there was some sort of a void. Although I loved poetry, I loved to argue too. Today, I regret not sticking with debate. Because of this I've reached the conclusion that you have to follow your heart and do what is best for you.

Despite this regret I must admit that our team was amazing, I mean, like what forensics (speech and debate) team can travel internationally and compete in Paris?

Not that many that I can think of.

We competed internationally against some of the top forensics schools in the United States. We placed fifth, but I walked away with no award. I was fine with that. I had no clue of what to expect, and this was my first year ever competing, but the experience in itself was the blessing. We went to the Eiffel tower, the Louvre, a variety of historical museums, tours, we even tried baguettes and even escargot. Traveling to Paris was fate. Purely, because the initials of Paris International Airport are C.D.G. And coincidentally my initials are C.D.G. Don't judge me! Also, Paris was one of the best experiences of my life. My life completely changed and my ideologies concerning higher education rose to another level.

Attending Mt. Sac, allowed me to realize the ample amount of resources that many people, like foster youth and first generation students are unfamiliar with. Because of it I am an avid advocate, supporter, proponent and spokesperson for students that may not have the financial backing to go to a university. Or for those who may need a second chance at school to take the transfer route.

Traveling meant the world to me. From being a little boy born in a jail cell to now traveling across the country, I've experienced something that was unprecedented, especially in my family. I was the first in my family to travel out of the country. I *actually* had a passport. You couldn't tell me nothing. It was such a rewarding experience that can never be taken away. My advice to my mentees, my nieces and nephews, brothers, sisters, cousins and to all of my college students, especially foster youth, is to TRAVEL! Go see something different outside our own cities. Life, purpose and our worth is more than just staying in a box! It is meant to be enjoyed to the fullest amount. As an emerging country currently battling racial tension and violence, we must experience other cultures and customs. We have to learn history.

Although I had one more year of eligibility left to compete on the forensics team, I couldn't. I had to say bye to Mt. Sac. I had a plan to transfer and I had to stick with it. My plan was to finish all my courses in one year at Mt Sac to transfer to UCLA. And I did just that, with honors. I became a recipient of the TAP Wasserman Scholarship. I applied to UCSB, UCI, UC Berkeley and UCLA. I got into them all. I thought about attending Berkeley, but I didn't want to move back up north. I wanted to move to Santa Barbara too because the school literally sits on a beach. But my mind was quickly made up to attend UCLA because all of that was not a part of the vision God had given me at 16 years old.

I always imagined that I would be at UCLA. But to actually be on the campus, living a dream come true, and making moves was something surreal. It was really happening. I remember getting the email saying I got accepted. I leaped, shouted and praised God for something that once was a dream, now had become a reality.

When God gives you a plan. . .

When you set something in your mind to accomplish, you must act on it!

Do not doubt it. Do not just talk about it, but be about it!

Being at UCLA had been a journey. After working for five years in the healthcare industry I told myself if I can put five years into a company that only viewed me as a number I could surely invest five years into my own education. I wanted to experience a part of my life as a full time student, and not to work while doing so. So for the first year I signed up to live in the dorms. I got assigned The Gardenia transfer hall, this dormitory was full of transfers from community colleges from all over the world. We were able to build a community. I was able to build lasting relationships. Most people I met there I still stay in contact with to this very day.

I was so ready to get to UCLA. I wanted to move in a few days early. So that first week I signed up to be a move in assistant. As a result of my decision I met two hardworking brothers Javan and Idriss. Instantly we formed a bond that we still have today. Together we became a part of the residential housing government. This was one of the many clubs and organizations that I joined.

Being at UCLA, or any top tier university can be overwhelming. There were so many newer faces. There were many unfamiliar resources. It is different than the community college life. While I thrived at the community college level and was a part of one of the top community colleges in the world, I was nervous at UCLA.
There I knew only a handful of people. But being the extrovert and the life of the party, I sought out for everything that would help me at school and later into my career. I joined the Black Bruin Transfers Success (BBTS) Program and served as the financial aid chair for two years. Then I tried out and made the award winning UCLA Mock Trial Team and became a thriving team member. We traveled all over California, to Arizona, and out of the state to compete. It was one of the best experiences of my life. But it was not speech and debate so I decided to leave it alone for the next few years. I joined the Bruin

Guardian Scholars program designed for foster youth and former foster youth and received a positive support system from Terriel Cox, and Brianna Harvey.

As a transfer student you only have two years at UCLA to maximize your time. I knew I had to do all that I could to set me up for success after I graduated. I knew that I was going to go to law school, so I joined a Pre-Law Fraternity - Kappa Alpha Pi Co-ed Pre-Law Fraternity, also known as KAPi. Although I joined for the professionalism, I stayed for the brotherhood. My big, Brian became a mentor for me. Even though I was order I did not allow my age to hinder me from learning from younger folks. I found this as a way to stay in tune with this generation. I think this is what adds value to me being a great Youth and Young Adult Pastor. People that are older, feel that they know everything, and cannot learn from those younger than them. The reality is we all can always learn something new from anybody at any time.

One highlight of my UCLA career was that I went to the Capitol in Washington D.C. with the Chancellor and twelve other student leaders for an advocacy trip. It was a jammed packed experience over winter quarter that changed my life. We stayed in the University of California (UC) housing, we went to the Human Rights Campaign (HRC), visited the department of education and we even met with senators and different congressmen and congresswomen to talk about a host of hot political topics. Our cohort was the first ones to do the trip for underprivileged students. Afterwards we advocated that UCLA keep the trip going. As a result of this advocacy, students that normally may not have had a chance to lobby or advocate are now able to represent UCLA in D.C.

I was fortunate to do two study abroad programs. The first one was summer 15' and was with the Political Science department to London, Brussels, Amsterdam and Paris. The second program was summer 16' which was with the Sociology department to Cuba. Both programs allowed a young Black boy that was born in a county jail to travel outside of the United States and experience life on a whole new level and gain a global perspective.

Even though I gained new perspective while attending UCLA I struggled a lot. I struggled with making friends on campus. Mt. Sac was a great school that set a great foundation but to go to a top tier school where academia celebrities existed was intimidating. I struggled with there being so much to do at UCLA. Mainly because doing one thing was something I was not too fond of. I wanted my hands in everything so I could learn and gain more experiences.

I struggled with adjusting to the quarter system as well as the new level of writing. Especially with Sociology. To overcome struggling with sociology, I formed a sociology group with Tova, Michael, Thomas, Noreen. We helped each other get through the two years. Because of our efforts and tenacity we all graduated in the two year time frame.

To further alleviate the struggles, I was experiencing, I picked up a minor in African American studies. Though this minor I learned about my people. I learned about respectability politics, Black politics, the great migration, urban sociology, heteronormative patriarchy, the prison industrial complex, mass incarceration, Black resistance, Black Liberation and so many other topics. These topics were unfamiliar because we were never taught Black history in k-12 curriculum beyond Martin Luther King Jr. (MLK). Learning about MLK was amazing, but so was learning about what has and was impacting my communities. What I learned empowered me to not quit. It also helped me to beat the odds of sociological theory, which was the worst class ever.

I was blessed to graduate in 2016 with a Bachelors of Arts in Sociology and minor in African American Studies. I just knew that I was going to law school. So I thought I could study three months and then take the LSAT, which is one of the hardest test I took in my life, without no problem. I was wrong. I left the LSAT testing center thinking I did great but when I got the results I cried. Because if you know anything about taking the LSAT, a 139 is one of the worst scores one could receive. I knew that I would barely get into any law school especially the ones I wanted to attend.

I had to search for a plan B. Because I knew me. If I was to hop into the working force, I would find myself not wanting to come back to school. I ended up looking online and still applying to the best law schools, including Harvard, Stanford, USC and UCLA. UCLA had a joint MA/JD program that was a blessing in disguise. I was fortunate to get accepted into the MA program but denied to the JD program. However, it worked in my favor. Being fortunate to stay at UCLA and research and write about something that is dear to my heart allowed me to flourish into someone I did not see myself becoming.

I remember my first day of graduate class. It was an urban education class that dealt with public policy. I remember feeling levels of fear, intimidation and unworthiness which caused me to doubt I belonged there. But in the back of my mind I could hear God telling me "do you not know who you are!?!"

I quietly excused myself from the class, stepped outside and took a self-empowering moment to tell myself " You got this!" Sometimes there won't be people around us to encourage us, so, we have to learn how to encourage ourselves. It feels weird at first but the reality is you are your best supporter! Never forget this!

Now Let's Uncover your dreams

Dreams: Everyone has them but one reason why there is no execution is because of the failure to write down a clear plan. List your goals.

Write down your dreams

_____
_____
_____
_____
_____
_____
_____
_____
_____
_____
_____

Write down your visions

_____
_____
_____
_____
_____
_____
_____
_____
_____
_____
_____

Why is your dream important?

_____
_____
_____
_____
_____
_____
_____
_____
_____
_____
_____

Don't give up on your dreams. No matter how long it takes to achieve them keep moving forward! Dream big! Aim big! Do it BIG!

CHAPTER 8:

WESTWOOD, CA

When I was a child, I spake as a child, I understood as a child, I thought as a child: but when I became a man, I put away childish things. - 1 Corinthians 13:

According to its mission statement, The Guardian Scholars Program was designed to assist former foster youth, focusing on support services for undergraduate and graduate students.

January 2018, I started and completed the best thing for my life yet; I went vegan for thirty-one days. This included 21 days of fasting with my church. I came back from a two-week vacation of self-discovery and God told me to complete this mission. No meat, no Instagram, going to the gym, new diet and more of the Word. Guacamole, salsa, salads, black beans, fruits, veggies and water became my friends. Discipline became my partner and having the willpower to say NO became my best friend.

This season of my life and yours, will require more of saying NO! But how? Especially, when you hate disappointing people. When people invite me to events, my initial thought is that I can go for thirty minutes or an hour and then leave, right? And then I end up staying for three hours or until the event closes. I always think that if I do say no then there is a possibility that they would not want to be friends with me anymore. This is something I found myself facing on a daily and weekly basis. I had to learn to say no. You have to learn how to say no!

No, I could not make a certain networking opportunity.
No, I can't give you any money to borrow.
No, I can't be your friend.

The year 2018 required more. I wanted to go to the next level. I knew first hand that each year and each season required something different in order to go to the next level.

The next level does not come with ease either. Growing up in church, the preachers would always say "new levels, new devils." This means when you go to another level, another temptation or desire will arise that require more discipline. I found myself in 2017, before starting our new millennial services, living this statement out.

I had fell victim to the "gram." Instagram, turned me into a self-loathing, self-gratifying individual again. Yes, even as a preacher of the gospel. I found myself hopping from one picture to the next and "hearting" them. I found myself in-boxing and in the "dms" of people I knew were potentially bad. I also found others in-boxing me, hoping they had a chance in my bed. My desires for certain people allowed options on both sides of the spectrum. I started to be drawn into a desire, a new devil, that would drive me to become what I could not allow. A man of lust. Because of this, it was critical that I go on the fast in 2018. I needed to break some things once and for all.

January 2018 was the perfect time to do it. At Living Faith Cathedral ("LFC") my team and I- consisting of Shannon, Devin, Jocelyn, Kim, Kym, Renada, Ashley, Deon, Thais, Brittney, and many others- did something that had never been done at LFC, we launched our own millennial service. This service was a weekly worship service for those ages 12 through 36.

The theme of our first millennial services was "generational curses." I knew one generational curse I needed to break off of my family was lust for sure. Lust for power, lust for sex, lust for success. Why? Lust can drive a person to becoming entangled with the wrong person or entertaining an outlandish idea. My mother loved sex and money. I loved sex and money. I knew that this was something I wanted to break once and for all.

What I discovered through my process of breaking the generational curse of lust was that my success was not actually tied to it. For the first time in my life I discovered my career of becoming the success story I am today was because of genuine encounters with both men and women. I came to realize that these men and women, who didn't lust after me or I after them, had led me to truly understanding my worth.

From that single millennial service on lust, and that fast period, I realized my worth extended beyond my generational curse of lust. Even though I came to this realization I have no regrets concerning the "new devils" I had faced. I do not believe in regrets. James 1:2 (ESV) teaches us to "Count it all joy, my brothers, when you meet trials of various kinds." Therefore, there is no need to regret the trials we face.

Living Faith Cathedral (LFC) has been one of the biggest highlights and transformative experiences of my life. Serving there as the Youth and Young Adult Pastor has been the one place that kept me centered. We all have things that can impact how we live on a day to day basis. From life problems, to school, and work problems. There has to be something that keeps us motivated. Thankfully for me, LFC aided in keeping me motivated.

It is easy to complain. It is easy to second guess ourselves. It is easy to give up. It is easy to quit. For some of us, it is easy to walk away from things and people. For myself, growing up with no parents, losing my grandparents as a teenager, and then going into the foster care system,

I found myself over the years easily quitting people and jobs because I felt like I had no true connection. But thankfully, LFC gave me the connection I needed.

As a Youth and Young Adult Pastor, I've learned that connections are extremely important. Because of this, millennials today need to be careful of whom we connect with. Like the saying says "birds of the same feather, flock together" or "you are who you hang with." These sayings aren't just sayings. They are actually true statements that we need to not only comprehend, but sit on. The reality is that everyone is not meant to be your friend. Everyone is not meant to be in your circle. Everyone is not meant to be in your life forever. And that is ok.

Who would have known that the connection to LFC would have been so vital to my life a couple of years later? When I moved back to Southern California I became Youth and Young Adult Pastor at LFC. At that time, I lived in Claremont, CA and was in my first year at Mt. Sac. I commuted every weekend taking the 215 to the 15 to the 138 to get to church. Then when I transferred to UCLA in 2014, I traveled back and forth from Westwood on the 405 every weekend to attend church. All so that I could maintain this connection.

While I did sometimes wish I resided in Lancaster, I realized that the hour plus drive to and fro allowed me some "me" time. I realized that the 2 hours I traveled each weekend, all so that I could maintain this connection, allowed me to focus in on what I needed to finish and accomplish. The bottom line is that nobody's perfect. But every day in every way our goal should be to work to be the best person we can be.

It was on those drives I learned in order for me to make ministry and school work, I had to have a strong team. So I strategized and put together a perfect team that not only helped me but strengthened my connection with LFC. My team consists of Gina Evans, John Stewart Jr, Shaura Smith (a.k.a Mickey). They have all proven to be my rocks. When I am not able to teach Bible study, Gina has my back by teaching.

Mickey, acting as my secretary, gets all the administrative things done for me. And J.R, my mentee, picks up wherever I may be lacking. He's often there doing one of the hardest jobs in ministry, raising funds.

Not only did my team help me as a Youth and Young Adult Pastor, but my family did as well. My nephews Darion, Darius, DJ and my niece Brianna helped guide, mentor, work, gather, witness, worship and pray over the ministry. Although they knew firsthand how hard it can be to work with me, they remained consistent and dedicated to the vision. This by itself was shocking because as pastor's kids, they knew the detriments and trauma church can place upon a family. I guess we were able to survive because of something my grandmother always said to us, "a family that prays together, stays together."

Let's Uncover your triggers
Triggers are everywhere. We all have them.
What are yours?

_____
_____
_____
_____
_____
_____
_____
_____
_____
_____
_____
_____

What are some steps you take when faced with them?

_____
_____
_____
_____
_____
_____
_____
_____
_____
_____
_____

If you haven't taken any steps to avoid them, what steps can you take?

_____
_____

Learning your triggers are vital to your success. Don't be afraid to not only learn them but to take steps to overcome them.

CHAPTER 9:

UNCOVER YOUR WORTH

———————— ❦ ————————

The steps of a good man are ordered by the Lord: and he delighteth in his way.
- Psalms 37:23

Moreover whom he did predestinate, them he also called: and whom he called, them he also justified: and whom he justified, them he also glorified. What shall we then say to these things? If God be for us, who can be against us?
-Romans 8: 30, 31

According to the npr.org, there are approximately 438,000 foster youth in America.

I was born in a prison.
I was molested.

I never met my biological mother and my biological father.

I was in the foster care system.

I was not the best teenager, battled with heavy emotional trauma.

I was angry, confused and distraught.

I overcame many obstacles.

The biggest obstacle, called living!

Whether your journey starts in jail, prison, legal custody, foster care or alone, in order to get to YOUR promise, you have to appreciate the process. Every step that has happened or taken place has happened for a reason. Sometimes we get answers quickly but other times we have to learn what true patience means. Within these trials and tests our true worth is further pushed, developed and thus becomes more important. One's perception of themselves can either make or break them. So, now what do we do with this understanding, hopefully gained through this book?

As a sociologist, youth pastor, activist, and future politician and lawyer I plan to change policy. Legislation and policy has driven our country to all time disgrace. Number 45 and his misconceptions and egregious false accusations of who deserves and who does not deserve to be here in the United States is something that everyone needs to take serious. Historical oppression and marginalization of ethnic communities have not been included in the public and normative discourse both in and out of school books. It is time to change the narratives that these universities research and include.

Black communities, because there is more than just one, agendas need to be pushed and expressed everywhere. However, the problem with building anything is that there will always be an indifference of opinions. But within this, one must learn to agree to disagree, as long as everyone is "eating." Families and communities have been forced to live paycheck to paycheck. Their desires for more, to become just economically independent, becomes exhaustive. This ideal of an American dream becomes a lost page in the book. They use to say the best way to hide something from negroes was to put it in a book.

Reading for Blacks was considered a privilege. If you were granted the privilege to read it was for the Master's benefit. You read the Bible to your congregation of slaves. The Bible was used as a tool of oppression but also a tool of freedom. The white man hated Black lives. #Blacklivesmatter was nonexistent in the 1800s until 2013 when the movement began. Instilling fear into the Black minds, bodies, and souls through the institution of white supremacy is what America was built upon. The killing of Native Americans and the enslavement of Africans is what built America to the great power it is now. Americans thought they lost their tradition, their value and their worth but Africans, Blacks displayed resilience at all times.

People ask "why do you go so hard?" I tell my nieces, nephews, mentees and people I encounter all the time that I am here to push them into a greater person, human and spirit. We all are born with innate "good" and "bad" abilities. We all have the desire to be great. However, we simply just don't know how to get there.

This book was intended to encourage every reader to appreciate their hardships, learn from them and become the best person they can be. There is no specific road map. It is made up as you go. The longer you live, the more detailed the map will become, with various destinations of cities and states that have helped shaped you into the worthy being that you are today. No one will truly understand you! Therefore, you are the only one that can place the value of your worth! Whether it be high or low? The decision is yours. . .

I have never been the conformer. So, what I have decided to do with the remaining pages is to place some of my best writings that I turned in at UCLA. I wanted to share the process of my story. UCLA was not the easiest school to navigate but I made the best of it. I will be able to leave the school knowing that I did all that I could to make it the best possible. I will be able to leave impacting generations to come. My worth extends beyond just me but it extends into the generations to come.

As a person of color and someone that identifies as Black, I realize that not everyone is put at the same level playing field so it is my duty and obligation to give back. That comes in various forms. One is this book and another with these writings so that people that's reading this can understand the level of writing and research that is expected from this university. We all are geniuses. Let me say that again for the person in the back, WE ALL ARE GENIUSES! It is not just for Albert Einstein to be labeled this. It is up to us to tap into our full potential and find the worth that is hidden within each one of us. It is there, now it is up to you to find it, make a plan and execute it.

I did it.

So can you!

<u>Here are my 10 TIPS for navigating a Higher Education Institution:</u>

1. Build Networks- join a club or organization
2. Research your institution
3. Go to office hours for both your Professors and Teacher Assistant.
4. Run for an office
5. Get to know your institutions administrators
6. Look for scholarships and funding
7. Give back and volunteer
8. Travel Abroad
9. Read as much as you can! Take notes
10. HAVE FUN

PART III

WRITING SAMPLE

Writing #1 - 1st Quarter of my Junior Year (First Year at UCLA) - 2014-2015

Christian Green
Professor Tyson, TA- Jessica Lee
November 24, 2014

The Advanced Vision of Black Feminism and its Contribution to the Struggle for the Democratic Ideal

Over the years, the lives and contributions of powerful thinking and effectively acting Black Feminists have provided an advanced vision both in theory and practice of what the true "democratic ideal" is and how that ideal can be best brought into reality. In just researching the topic of Black Feminism in the Freedom Movement going back even before the end of slavery, I was overwhelmed with the dozens of names representing lives dedicated to the "democratic ideal" within the movement toward racial equality.

I could not possible dive into all of these lives and their individual contributions.

So, I will concentrate on a selected few of the past as well as current women that I can see as strong Black Woman who didn't and don't suffer themselves to be accepting of a second position in humanity because of their gender or their race or both.

Though totally varied in terms of their contributions to Black Freedom and feminist reputations, women such as **Sojourner Truth, Harriet Tubman, Amy Jacques Garvey,** Rosa Parks, Ella Baker, Angela Davis, and even in popular culture of Oprah Winfrey and Beyoncé are names thought of when people think of black feminism or black feminist thought in history and today's society.tc

It is no accident that the subtitle of our Text on Ella Baker written by Barbara Ransby, *Ella Baker and the Black Freedom Movement* is subtitled: *A Radical Democratic Vision.* In one of her commencement addresses she spoke to the students and talked about what it means to be a "radical" or have a "radical" analysis. She pointed out that radical traditionally means to get to the "root." I recalled that the same is true in mathematics, the symbol for the root of a number is the radical, i.e.,

Thus, looking at the root of the ideal of "democracy," which by definition means the rule by the majority, where political power is exercised by each person's vote as 1 out of the total population. Analyzing deeper toward the root, we see that for democracy to work, everyone (every human being) has to have an <u>equal</u> say, regardless of any characteristic that would differentiate that person from any other person.

This right to an equal say, is based upon equal human rights with all other human beings. Whatever rights one has must also be available to every other human being. Thus the power of the majority has to be limited, in that the majority cannot use their power, to deny the political minority their equal access to human rights and equality. Thus, we have all of this at the foundation of democratic theory. It goes without saying that if the "few" rule, and exploit the majority (which is a necessary condition of capitalist) there is no democracy, but an oligarchy or plutocracy.

So this democratic ideal as was stated at the foundation of the U.S. with the Declaration of Independence, where it states: "We hold these truths to be self-evident, that all men [as human kind] are created equal, that they are endowed by their Creator with certain unalienable Rights, that among these are Life, Liberty and the pursuit of Happiness." This concept, at least in principle, has now been reasserted throughout the world much more recently in the "Universal Declaration of Human Rights," as adopted by the United Nations and now a part of International Law.

Between these two declarations came the assertion of a "Classless Society" by Karl Marx that in its final ideal form, would provide for total equality of each person as well. Essentially the same thing as the "Democratic Ideal." The radical insight of Marx's criticism of capitalist economics is that free enterprise competition, by its nature leads to "winners" (the few) and "losers" (the majority) in terms of wealth and power. If there is no restraint the few use their power to dominate the many and take away their equal rights for the benefit of the few. So, this inequality of class undermines the goal of the democratic ideal.

Ella Baker's ideas reflected this, and in this sense she was a student of Marx or at least Marxian principles. She would apply the analysis of a classless society to her position supporting the rule by the majority through a struggle by the majority (have nots) against domination (denial of human rights) by the few (haves) who hold power over the majority. That is also why her model for activism also tended to be from the bottom up, instead of relying on the charismatic leadership from the top down. (Ransby, Page 74)

Likewise, it would also be illegitimate for or any group to rule (minority OR majority) that disrespected the inherent equal human rights of any other human beings. She combined Marxist theory with Baptist missionary values that advocated for a redistribution of society's wealth and a transfer of power from capitalist elites to the poor and working class. She was a grassroots organizing radical who had class privilege and a higher education that graduated from Shaw Academy.

"Baker recognized that aspects of her background- her class privilege, higher education, residence in New York City, and close contact with prominent national leaders- made her different from many of the uneducated folk she worked with in the South. Nevertheless, she did not want those differences to overshadow their commonalities" (Ransby, p. 113)

She believed that the patterns of correcting racial, social and political injustices of the African American required the inclusion of the impoverished and poor together with the middle class of society. (Ransby, p. 74)

Coming from this viewpoint, Ella Baker puts the Black Freedom Movement into this struggle to achieve "true" democracy in a radical form not always appreciated by those leaders with less vision or confidence in the people and the movement. This movement goes beyond the rights of a particular group of people, but by necessity must include all. Therefore her approach in many ways was visionary in terms of the Black Freedom Movement in terms of its great social, political, and economic promise as a world changing purpose in history, which was not limited in its spirit:

Even if segregation is gone, we will still need to be free; . . .
Remember, we are not fighting for the freedom of the Negro alone,
but for the freedom of the human spirit, a larger freedom that
encompasses all of mankind.
(Ransby, Barbara. *Ella Baker & The Black Freedom Movement: A Radical Democratic Vision*, p. 319)

For many years in the south, abuse of black women has always ran rapid. For many years, black women would have to deal with abuse, molestation and rape. Rape by men both in public and private setting was implanted as a "weapon of terror" (McGuire, preface xviii) to kill the human spirit of the Black Woman. They used this "weapon of terror" to instill fear in the Black woman and the Black man. Recy Taylor, a victim of gang rape, Rosa Lee Cherry who was walking home, was threatened by three police officers if she did not get in, was raped, and Lila Belle Carter, a 16 year old never escaped, an insurance collector abducted, raped and murdered her when she was on her way back from getting her mother some rice. These horrific and evil real life events happened when a time when black women, rape and resistance were making history of the civil rights movement while also advocating with only a nonviolent retaliation movement.

" Verbal, physical and sexual abuse maintained racial hierarchy in an enclosed space where separation of whites and blacks was all but impossible. A big arrow pointing to the rear of the bus for "colored" and another pointing to the front of the bus for whites provided some guidance. This policy fueled resentment and anger among African Americans, especially domestics and day laborers who spent hours on their feet cooking. While abuses piling up like cordwood and memories of previous crimes smoldering, a group of black women decided to take on the bus drivers by demanding to be treated like ladies. The Women's Political Council led the charge". (McGuire, Danielle. *At the Dark End of the Street*.)

The historical struggle for fair treatment of public transportation through multiple Bus Boycotts before the famous Montgomery Alabama bus when Rosa Parks "Didn't give up her seat. These movements more was powerful and symbolic than one could imagine for the African American Women. Alice Walker, Rosa Parks, Black feminist theorists such as Angela Davis, Bell Hooks and Patricia Hill Collins have all fought against being marginalized more than white women along the lines of race, class, gender and sexuality.

"Although we are feminists and Lesbians, we feel solidarity with progressive Black men and do not advocate the fractionalization that white women who are separatists demand. We struggle together with Black men against racism, while we also struggle with Black men about sexism." (Combahee River Collective Statement)

The Combahee River collective was anti-capitalist and operated under a different approach than the social views of the National Black Feminist Organization (lecture notes). They wanted to transform movements within the black community as well as movements within other women.

"We realize that the liberation of all oppressed peoples necessitates the destruction of the political-economic systems of capitalism and imperialism as well as patriarchy."

(Combahee River Collective Statement)

Black feminism in today's society would want to end a dominate floor. The idea is to lift the floor for everyone, but not by necessarily breaking the ceiling to be above (more powerful than) others. But causing a shift including social growth and maturity recognizing other ideas that did not reflect a "European" capitalist base. Many African American Feminists have turned to Africa to search for the old social and political societies which reflected the reality of honoring social and collective needs. (See:, For example, Patricia Hill Collins in her work: *Black Feminist Thought.*)

These ideas are sought to offer an alternative to the mythologies supporting unrestrained individual "liberty" to dominate others in the fierce "survival of the fittest" mythologies basic to capitalism and European sociological theories like those of Weber, who recognized, if not admired, the role of the "protestant ethic" and ideas like "predestination" particularly in American capitalism as a "rationalization" of slavery and racism and gender discrimination. (From my readings in Sociological Theory, for example Weber, Max. *The Spirit of Capitalism,* p. 138)

If and when all Americans, all races, genders and social class agreed with the "grassroots" methodology of Ella Baker it would provide awareness on how to understand social, gender and race conflicts in the fight for the "ideal" democracy. Who would have known that while Ella Baker was not just fighting against the white bus driver who would attempt to "put her in her place" when she, like all black people, in the south, was also fighting against male politics within her own establishment of work, the NAACP. She was determined to stand up for herself at the same time and she stood up for her sex, her race, and those at the bottom of the social and economic hierarchy.

As Americans, we must realize that it cannot be allowed to be about our race, gender or socio economic status, because we are supposed to be created equal. If everyone had the beliefs of a black feminist, the world would be ideal and might be able to attain the Democratic Ideal. But without the comprehensive approach of the Black Feminist movement, it is not likely to happen and to any less comprehensive alternative, the Combahee Collective would not be so easily convinced: "We are not convinced, however, that a socialist revolution that is not also a feminist and anti-racist revolution will guarantee our liberation." (Combahee River Collective)

Bibliography

Collins, Patricia Hill. *Black Feminist Thought.* Routledge (1991).

Combahee River Collective. Combahee River Collective Statement. See online: http://circuitous.org/scraps/combahee.html

Little, Anita. How many of these early black feminists do you know? *"Ms. Blog."* (February 19, 2014) Viewed online: http://msmagazine.com/blog/2014/02/19/how-many-of-these-early-black-feminists-do-you-know/

McGuire, Danielle. *At the Dark End of the Street.* Vintage Books (2010).

Randsby, Barbara, *Ella Baker and the Black Freedom Movement: A Radical Democratic Vision.* University of North Carolina, 2003.

Weber, Max. *The Spirit of Capitalism.* London: Routledge. (1997).

Writing #2 - Senior Year, UCLA 2015-2016

Christian Green
Professor R. Rocco
Poli Sci 119 Final

The Political Consciousness of Cuba

Fidel Castro on July 26th 1959, during their revolutionary movement, stated "History will absolve me!" This statement was revolutionary to their fighting against colonialism, oppression and marginalization so that there would be a sense of national identity. Although the statement is only four words, it will make sense later to the people of Cuba and to the world. His statement is metaphorically applicable to the four writers that we will discuss in this paper. Castro, accredited the famous writers and especially the revolutionary, socialist, and leader Jose Marti, but also these other writers with helping the revolution movement ideology, thus changing the Cuban economy, identity and essentially the "Nuestra Americas." In order for people to understand the political consciousness and identity that lies within Cuba, one must examine the historical contexts and ideologies of the associated writers. In this essay we will examine four different thinkers, Simon Bolivar, Jose Marti, Leopoldo Zea and Paulo Friere, each from different periods, but interestingly they all similarly pursued a common goal of critically analyzing the current time, ideologies, and teachings in order to gain political, cultural and mental independence, liberty and consciousness for the people of Cuba, ultimately contesting the Euro Western thoughts regarding colonization and ideology and forming the conception of the "Nuestras America" through the idea of independence.

The long lasting effects of colonization from the Western thoughts and ideology include oppression, marginalization, domination, power, control, coercion, and intimidation just to name a few effects. These effects were instrumental in how these four writers framed and constructed their theories. Simon Bolivar wrote in the early 19th century and Jose Marti wrote in the late 19th century. Leopoldo Zea wrote in the mid 20th century and Paulo Friere wrote in the mid to late 20th century. All of these timeframes were centered around wars and slavery, but all these times dealt with specific problems detailing certain economic tragedies in which we will discuss during each writer's ideological thinking and analysis.

The first writer, Simon Bolivar, frames his work around political independence to help the theme of "Nuestra America" emerge from the relationship between colonization and independence. He was one of the major architects of the Latin America War of Independence against Spain during the 19th century. Bolivar believed in absolute legal equality for all individuals no matter their class, creed or color. His political thought included the notion of "poder moral" which was the need to cultivate the development of politcal culture of tolerance and civility. His political thought also was a mixture of theoretical arguments and practical proposals, which included three phases of ideology.

Bolivar's three phases of ideology are 1) Winning the war of the independence, implicating a revolution; 2) Once the war is one, they need to figure out how to handle independence; and 3) Unite the entire republic. Now, although Bolivar rejected federalism, he still wanted to build a federation through creating an indigenous concept of democracy. His normative goal was to achieve liberty and equality through creating a Pan-American federation of individual democratic republics based on federalism, democracy and racial mixture (mestizo). However, Bolivar faced many challenges with implementing this new mindset and he acknowledged that and built upon it. He faced the legacy of colonialism, political fragmentation, cultural domination, and economic underdevelopment. He faced a heterogenous population which was the need for mestizo population. There was a huge racial divide including years of slavery which contradicted the democratic governance, and which ultimately perpetuated ineffective forms of governance. Bolivar knew that this was an issue that would take a long time to dismantle.

Therefore, Bolivar implemented a broad strategy to dismantle the physical and mental effects of years of colonialism. His strategies were to 1) Develop strong governmental structures and authority. 2) Eliminate the caudillo system of power. 3) Promote the notion of national identity to replace the form of colonized consciousness. 4) To eliminate slavery and lastly, 5) Develop international political alliances and economic ties. Bolivar once stated "Liberty is the only object worth the sacrifice of a man's life, not simply freedom from absolutism but freedom from colonial power." Bolivar ultimately wanted to help create a sense of identity for the "Nuestra America" and it was Jose Marti that encouraged a sense of a natural type of cultural identity.

Our second writer, Jose Marti played an instrumental role in the development of the Cuban identity and ultimately laid the foundation for the Cuban Revolution of 1878. His main ideology was Cuban Nationalism, meaning a common political identity among the Cuban people. Marti believed the goal was to promote the emergence of what he called "real" man authenticity expression of Latin America, which embodied "Nuestra America." Marti stated "Nations that do not know one another should quickly become acquainted, as men who are to fight a common enemy. Those who shake their fists, like jealous brothers coveting the same tract of land, or like the modest cottager who envies the esquire his mansion, should clasp hands and become one."

Marti believed that in order for his notion of "Nuestra America" to become a reality that a transformation of beliefs and practices that spanish colonization had imposed for 300 years that required a close study of the histories of " Nuestra America." He believed that the futures of the these societies within the "Nuestra America" depended on the developing institutions, principles, forms of government and economic relations that were indigenous to the countries of "Nuestra America." Marti's normative foundation was built on three concepts of liberty, justice and equality.

Marti, the leader of the Cuban Revolutionary Party believed that winning the war of independence from Spain was an immediate task for the party to gain liberty, justice and equality. Even more so, wanted a long-term role in transforming mindsets and eliminating the negative influences and characteristics that the Cuban society inherited after 300 years of colonization. Marti felt there was a need for a political identity and that with eliminating the spanish colonial system, that it needed to be replaced with a republican democracy like Bolivar's ideology. Both Bolivar and Marti knew that after gaining independence that the people would need help with transforming their mindsets from a colonized state. However, in comparison to Bolivar, Marti believed that there needed to be a republican democracy based on freedom and justice that incorporated all classes and not just the elites. He also believed that there was no need to borrow principles from other nations, but that there was a need for an indigenous government. Marti termed "el hombre natural" for those who create and organized against spanish rule and they have to overcome "el libro importado" and los letrados articiales." Marti, ultimately believed that there was a need to create a natural cultural identity which in return would help the colonized get away from the long lasting negative physical and mental effects of the colonizer.

Leopoldo Zea asserted a radical egalitarian framework and believed that dependency and marginalization played a critical role in understanding the colonized and the colonizer, similarly to Marti. He looks at three dimensions or levels in the analysis of cultural identity. He first looked at the relation between cultural identity and self-knowledge by focusing on Mexican national identity. Secondly, he looked at the relation between cultural identity and nationalism in how he engages in the history of Americas and offers a philosophy of American history. Lastly, he looked at the relation between cultural identity and liberation, Zea develops the interpretation of colonized imperialism. Mexico, Latin American Countries and all other colonized countries connected together and that marginalization and dependency were the defining characters between being colonized and the colonizer. Zea elaborates on the projects and stages and types of development of political stages within the Latin American history and argues that there were six major projects that represented distinct stages of American History: the Iberian colonizer, the occidental colonizer, the libertarian, the conservative, the civilizer, and the assimilative. This ideology of positivism was in place to agree or be consistent with the policy set in place to colonize the people.

Positivism was used with scientific thinking and we see this work with the apologists. They say clearly that this was the way to get away from our "Indian-ness" They stated that "we need to adopt the European traditions by using science." "This was a form of hatred; racism is still persistent in Mexico. However, Zea was opposed to this type of thinking. He incorporates a critique of what he considers the expansionist European culmination in the "colossus of the north" in the US. We are replicating what we are taught from the European version, which was the ultimate problem.

Zea went to the heart of this problem. Zea moved forward and dealt with the culture and self-knowledge. He looked into the dynamics and how positivism was not a great idea. Specifically in Mexico, positivism was the ideology. Positivism was used to justify dictatorship. However, Zea critiques this philosophy and draws to the alternative, three Mexican thinkers, one is Antonio Caso who elaborates on the humanist ethic, which asserts the personhood of each individual makes a person equally valued to every other person. He then draws on his second writer, Vasconcelos, who stands for the notion of a United Latin American community based on a vision of a blending of races and the notion of mestizaje (representing the best-in consists of three identities). Mexico was more mixed than any other country. They consisted of European, Indigenous, and Africans. The mixture represented the humanistic value. The emerging of the three people, Razas, produces mestizos, and Zea takes this idea that most Latin Americans are all three of these cultures, Vasconcelos celebrates this. The third thinker is Ramos who deals with the idea that political independence, political and economic development are, by themselves, not sufficient to promote true freedom. Ramos is asking a more fundamental question: where does this self-hatred come from?

Zea uses all these philosophers and principles from Mexico and sees how these dynamics and processes are all happening in the Americas but in a broader context. Zea said we can't move forward unless we accept it, we have to find the root, affirm it and recognize it. We are all damaged, but we have to be the agents to recognize it and advance forward. Even Malcolm X, in dealing with the blackness in America, questioned his blackness. He wanted to be white. He wanted to straighten his hair and bleached his skin because of what society made one feel. You could not be a part of society unless you were white. This self - hatred from the damage of slavery and colonization affects people from all over the world. He believes that all the colonized societies have been the object of the same, domination, dependency, marginalization and fragmented identities.

Lastly, Paulo Friere, the fourth writer, was another prominent and unique in his own right. He wrote wrote his work in the 1950s, 60s, 70s, and was problematic to a certain extent. His writing was different from the other three, they were concerned with colonization legacy. Bolivar refers to it, but his, Frieres, analysis is more concentrated on how to build latin federation. Marti, also deals with Cuban nationalism, its Latin American roots, but how they needed to build support for the revolution and to ultimately build an identity. However, he developed a critique of the existing ideology, but no pedagogy, what was the role of the revolution party? He set that up as the agent to address colonization. Marti understood there had to be a counter-narrative. He founded the revolutionary party which was originally in exile. Zea's intervention, looked primarily at building a counter narrative theory in philosophy by european theory of latin america. He wanted to intervene in a more academic way, and claims about universality dealing with colonization. They all have contributed to this ideal of identity but differently from Friere.

The difference with Friere was that he tried to create a more direct or specific theory, called pedagogy. He tried to develop a "how do you do it?" "How do you transfer the colonization consciousness" The difference has a more direct approach to the problem. He initially came to the method of literacy, and then the teaching of literacy. His main framework was developing a method/pedagogy for developing awareness or "conscientization" of the objective causes of domination. There are different types of Friere models of teachings. There is the horizontal (which relies on teaching the content, but trying to learn their own reality) vs vertical (the teaching of a particular ideology). The vertical results in hierarchy because they want you to learn their way. The horizontal model, if successful, you leave the job. You have to embed yourself in the organization of help.

He is dealing with european colonialism like the other three. He looks at the economic political and cultural marginalization. He is wondering the same things as are the other writers. But, he wants to look at how? He makes the distinction between the concepts of imperialism and colonialism. Colonialism is a form of imperialism in which an annexed territory are ethnically, racially and culturally different. Imperialism is state policy to establish or maintain political control over territories and peoples outside the state. Colonialism was a racial project. However, this was not the main focus. The colonizing project was the anglo and Iberian colonization--as we learned in lecture. .

Friere looks at Latin American Colonization, he argues that colonization resulted in colonized consciousness, the people basically inherited and internalized this form of historical consciousness. He explains that the ways you see yourself are built by the intellectuals or colonizers and that is how you develop your sense of self. Frieres is saying this is exactly what you need to undo the loss of self identity, thanks to racial and class domination. He believed that decolonization requires the development of a historical critical consciousness in place of the mystifying (false) colonization consciousness. It involves the quest for self identity. The project is this undoing and replacing of false consciousness, "conscientization," defined as the process of transforming mystifying consciousness into a historical critical consciousness. He develops his own normative framework.

His framework is based on the idea of an ontological vocation also known as Humanization. Humanization and depression basically means whatever prevents individuals from becoming more fully human limits inherent potential for human freedom. Freire argues that the goal of becoming humanized is becoming conscious of the causes of oppression, such political, economic inequality, poverty, discrimination, through reflection and praxis. Frieres really depended on education. Freire's concept of education refers to something different and much more profound, than is the common understanding of that term.

The concept of education depended on two types of education: banking and problem solving. Banking is when the teacher deposits the information and then withdraws information from the examinations. His banking education model is structured to impose a particular system of thought that has a specific content and is based on a hierarchical conception of teaching and learning process. His problem solving model is based on the goal of problematizing the natural environment. Emphasizing self discovered solutions through critical thinking and individual and creative discovery. It is structured to facilitate the process but not the content. His goal of this education is not to impart a specific process forcefully. This process incorporates some of the characteristics of both, but ultimately it is depended on Friere's pedagogy. His pedagogy revolves around three propositions. People should create a world where humanization replaces dehumanization, a world in which it is easier to love. People have the ability to create their world and be conscious of the capacity. The key elements of the literacy and pedagogical method is research, thematization and problematization.

His method of pedagogy is the methods that consists of a series of problems that exist every day. It is a series of problems to be solved. It is a collaborative process of critical problem solving and in that dialogue is central. The contrast to the banking method requires prepackaged bits of information deposited into the blank minds of the students. The model basically states that you cannot do this by yourself. You have to do it with others. This problem solving is dependent upon culture, praxis, science, social literacy, dialogue, culture of words/themes and problematization He refers to science as not being the dominate conclusion of culture. By dominating or decolonizing you have to learn yourself and be conscious of the society and earn their trust.

The type of social analysis for pedagogy requires lengthy community based research to discover thematic universe of cultural circle. The methods include ethnography, [participant observation, family and household interviews, interviews in sites of civil society, in example, sites of everyday experience]. It is also the need to understand how participants make sense of their experience. As a facilitator, the role is to understand the objective of the general world. You use the problem solving form of learning and rely on dialogue as a way of for participants to mutually interrogate each other's view of their experience and to discover that they conform to similar forms of oppression. The three problem sequence is: 1) name the important conflicts in the situation; 2) you have to understand the explanation; and 3) develop collaborative action to resolve the problems and conflicts. People who do not engage in this dialogue will not help in transformative power. People have to understand that they can change their situation, conditions and problems. The generative themes involve a central role of unequal power, it is central to a wide variety of specific conflicts, it reflects the central conflict of domination and implies its opposite, the theme of liberation.

1) in the naming of the conflict, one must discover the generative words chose to represent familiar conflict situations and by generative we mean that the facilitator can generate discussion by posing questions. 2) One must analyze the systemic cause of conflict you have the generative words, then the generative themes, then the central conflicts and then thematic universe. 3) Collaborative action to resolve the problems and conflicts. There has to a collaboratively naming and analyzing problems and conflicts through dialogue. It also is this process that is at the basis of problematizing the experience of the oppressed.

In Conclusion, all four of these writers try to debunk and decolonize the Anglo Saxon thinking, all from different time frames, but ultimately fighting for the same thing- a building of a Cuban culture identity and the rebuilding of "Nuestra America"

Ultimately, this trip to Cuba has been eye-opening and rewarding to say the least. I didn't realize that this country was faced with so many issues still resulting and damaged from the effects of being colonized. When I first came to Cuba I thought I was going see more black people in power, but as the writers mentioned above, whiteness seems to be the ideal type of skin color to engage or employ with. Although there are black people here working in ample amounts, there are not too many "dark" skinned people in control or in power. However, when we asked about race or racism, they all say there is no race or racism that exists here in the Cuba. However, in contrast we had a guest lecturer, Roberto Zurbano who said that there was definitely persistent racial disparities, injustices and conflicts. We were able to travel to Varadero, for the beach and spend some time out there to experience something else besides Havana. It was amazing, but something we did think was that because Cubans from Havana are allowed to go there only if they are invited was something weird.

Paper #3 - 1st Quarter of Grad School - Fall 2016-2017

Christian Green
Dr. Steven Nelson

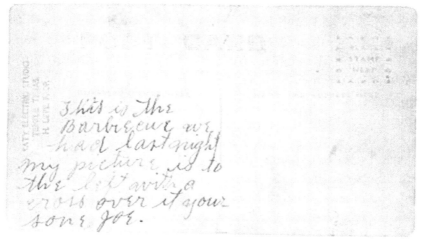

The Romanticism of Lynching Postcards (1900-1963)

"This is the barbeque we had last night. My picture is to the left with a cross over it sincerely, your son, Joe." (Allen, 26, Wood 108) This message was sent from a son who seemed proud of his role at the "dinner" to his parents. Egregious messages alongside pictures of black bodies being lynched were regularly sent on postcards to parents, friends, family, colleagues all over the country and all over the world. During the post reconstruction and emancipation period from the late 1800's until the pre-civil rights era, early 1960's, heinous, vilifying, evil images, language, messages and rhetoric degrading the black culture had become the norm and were widespread in the United States to promote white supremacy (Apel and Smith, 78). Today, in our current times of the early 21st century, "Picture Postcards" are looked at as being of some romantic sentimental value, something signifying honor or pride, or documenting a scene or venue or a commemorative event. They are not used today simply as one of the most pervasive, cheap and relatively convenient form of communication as they may have been in the early 20th century, but nevertheless and in both cases, these same characteristics remain an aspect of the image represented and a reflection of a romanticized perception of how physical, moral, or social "reality" ought to be perceived. It is consistent with the political socialization or cultural norms bought into, by the sender, the photographer, and publisher of the image purveyed (Apel, 151). In any case, what goes directly to the research question, which is examined in this paper, is why Picture Postcards, that depict black bodies burned to their bones or horribly tortured, maimed or hanging in death from the activities of lynch mobs of white folks, were so captivating or romanticized that white people paid extra for these post cards and the images depicted thereon, and then mailed them to friends and loved ones as if they were commemorating something good or to be proud of? What were these post-cards signifying or communicating? This project will also research the nature of the impact these commonly celebrated pictures postcard images of lynchings made on members of the black communities and what messages and meanings these postcards, as a subset of all widely used communication media during this timeframe, and whether it may have have been internalized by fellow African-Americans.

The development of Picture Postcards represented an economic boom and began to be widely used across the globe for social and political communication. UCLA Art History professor, Saloni Mathur, has reviewed and provided delicate and sensitive research involving the emergence of images and picture postcards made with the development of photography during the height of European Colonialism in Asia, the Middle East, and Africa. She researched the significance of postcards and images made by those in power over those in a subordinate power position in relations to the hierarchies of colonialism and the wounds induced by imposing the images the conquerors made of subordinate peoples as the definitive norm or accepted version of "reality," while ignoring the silence of those subordinated people photographed. One can only imagine that the human subjects, objectified in these images, would certainly have had a most different view of the "righteousness" of the romanticized views depicted in the photographic "eye" of the white supremacist and european colonizers. See, for example, the work of Malek Alloula, "The Colonial Harem" (First published in the U.S. in 1986). As colonial people gained their own voices out of their previous silence they ultimately began calling for their independence from their colonizers and in doing so were determined as Alloula asserted: "to return this immense postcard to its sender." Similarly, my research will try to understand: why postcards of lynchings were not immediately and with revolutionary zeal, "returned back to their sender," in the United States, but instead seemed romanticized, cherished and treasured looking back to and perpetuating a time of unchallenged legal, social, and "morally acceptable," racial inequality and white supremacy. A time of an unambiguous racial system where the "negro," in the common parlance of the time: "knew his place."

Coinciding with the post emancipation political and social need to reassert and affirm racial inequality among those white people who were resisting any actualization of universal human rights, came the development of photography and the means to reproduce photographs on printed paper and a cheap way to distribute these through the U.S. Mail. The periodical historical analysis shows that Austria became the first country to introduce the postcard in the year of 1869 (Mathur, 112). America, on February 21, 1871 the US Congress passed an act allowing that privately owned and produced printed cards can be mailed. Then, June 8, 1872, Congress passed legislation that approved government production of postal cards and the first were issued on May 1, 1873, almost a year later. One side of the postcard was for a message and the other side was for the recipient's   address. (http://siarchives.si.edu/history/exhibits/postcard/postcard-history ; 11/15/16)

Subsequently, these developments in "picture postcard distribution" were utilized to produce and widely distribute messages and photographic captions of lynchings, where black people were being massacred by fellow white citizens, their bodies beaten and ridiculed in front of both large and smaller crowds, a practice that became a craze in some communities in America.

Postcard publishers in both America and Europe struggled to meet the enormous "attraction of these persuasive little agent's." George Eastman's Kodak in 1888, had enabled and aided in this as they developed the means whereby "high-quality" photographic images could be printed directly on paper and thus cost effectively mass-produced and in doing so helped reshape the processes by which images were produced and consumed. (Mathur, 113) This photographic postcard became a new "social medium" of the day: a fad, a craze putting communities in this "frenzy." This "frenzy"of postcard activity was huge during the years of 1890 to 1918. (Mathur,114)   In France, picture postcard production was recorded as an estimated 8 million in 1899 and jumping to 60 million by 1902 and 123 million in 1910. In Britain, during 1908 more than 860 million cards were reported to have passed through the British post. In America in 1908 alone, more than 677 million picture postcards were sent. (Mathur, 114) Of course these astronomical numbers are not exclusively of lynchings or terrible images alone, but these and all the images do reflect the reality of social life, cultural norms and "tastes" of the time. This visual documentation brings home to us the horrible reality of the mentality of many in society of the time and the terror that they intentionally brought to African-Americans as one looks into the eyes and faces of all represented in the picture postcards.   The power of visual art is underscored as we are overwhelmed by these images, including the words of the handwritten messages scrawled upon them, compared, for example, to the relatively benign written statement of documentary prose in a history book that says: "an estimated 3,445 blacks died at the hands of lynch mobs between 1882 and 1968."

How did this society get to the place that is represented by the vulgarity of these images which document the reality of their time? The American Civil War "officially" ended in 1865 and "freedom" was proposed for the black communities. However, the reconstruction period was just that, a reconstruction and reassertion of past racial relationships based on the white imposed premise of racial inequality (Wood, 10). But, now that slavery was no longer legal or constitutional, what other ways could they find as being possible to hold the negro back in a subordinate position, oppressed and in service to the white economy. One answer lay in the very constitutional words that were meant to emancipate Blacks from slavery. So, after the civil war was over and primarily justified by claiming that African Americans were freed thereby, there remained a horrable and ominous paradox (Wood, 3). The 13th amendment stated that:

"Neither slavery nor involuntary servitude, except as a punishment for crime whereof the party shall have been duly convicted, shall exist within the United States, or any place subject to their jurisdiction."

The 13th Amendment was passed by Congress on January 31, 1865 and ratified by the states by the end of that same year, namely, December 6, 1865. The horrifying truth, however, was that, although this amendment abolished slavery and involuntary servitude, it retained these evils within certain specified exceptions, namely it retained slavery and involuntary servitude as a punishment imposed by government over its people when the government convicted such people of committing crimes. Therein lay a terrible problem for the negro subject of a white dominated former slave state government. After its adoption in 1865, there began a period of reassertion of racism and racial inequality including segregational practices, indentured servitude, peonage, and trumped up convictions for crimes, facilitating government leasing of convict labor to the private sector, thus giving rise for a means for white supremacy to continue to reign supreme in America and continue to benefit economically from free labor of African-American convicts (Wood, 8).

During the post-reconstruction period, there were thousands of lynchings that took place in the late 19th and early 20th centuries. This severe form of discipline allowed whites to beat, rape and lynch black people at any time without any penalty. Some mobs would take over jails and bring the "criminal" out before the public so everyone could see "what is done to a negro." (Apel and Smith, 11) But any critical analyst must ask, why was this allowed? And Why did few whites speak out against it? Lynchings were of the norm in southern states and some northern states during the early 20th century. Thousands of black bodies hung over lakes, bridges, on trees, or in community parks or spaces. They made a spectacle of it. They romanticized it.

As previously discussed, the morbid popularity of lynching postcards coincided with a larger postcard craze during the 1890's and World War I (Wood, 107). Postcards and photographs during these timeframes acquired meaning not through mass consumption but through individualized expression and sentiment. Although these picture postcards of lynchings appeared grotesque, it shows how the spectators of lynchings deemed these events as being both customary and spectacular. The photograph postcards were extensions of private photographs and a visual form of connection and communication between loved ones. Often, the senders would send personal messages on the back of the card and it would render a communal and commercialized event personal and intimate. Similar to the opening sentence of " This is the barbeque we had last Saturday." Joe Meyers marked the postcard of Jesse Washington charred body to show his parents where he was in the crowd. (Allen, 26 and Wood, 108)

This postcard image shows the aftermath of a 1920 Duluth, Minnesota lynching where three African-American circus workers falsely accused of raping a white woman were brutally murdered-- Lynched without trial. The three victims are surrounded by an all white crowd, dressed in their overcoats and warm hats, facing the photographer and posing for the camera. They are memorializing the killing, the murder, the death of these three falsely accused men, while two are hanging from a rope and the third on the ground laid out face down. These three have no shirts on, clothes were torn off and their skin bruised but yet the crowd shows no remorse when taking their photographic moment. This type of mockery was the norm in white dominant societies and not exclusively in the southern states, where, of course, most were carried out (Wood, 17).

This postcard image included the lynching of Laura Nelson and her son in Okemah, Oklahoma, May 25, 1911. These two are hanging over a river. The mother's dress looks as if it is blowing in the picture. These two are hanging under the bridge while a row of white men, women and children are standing overlooking them and appear to be posing for the picture. They are looking in admiration and glory at what had been done. White men thought of lynching as something heroic. They believed they were helping and protecting the white community by lynching and killing these black bodies, without legal justification or judicial order. The act itself is a reaffirmation of racial inequality and the application of the doctrine of white supremacy, regardless of law or the U.S. Constitution.

This postcard image includes the lynching of Thomas Shipp and Abram Smith in Marion Indiana on August 7, 1930. These two were accused of raping an eighteen-year-old white female and murdering her twenty-four-year-old boyfriend. Tom Shipp was nineteen and Abram Smith was eighteen. They were both dragged out of the jail by white mobs, attacked, beaten, stabbed, clubbed, dragged and lynched. " Along the way most of their clothes were torn off. When the white men dragging smith stopped briefly, several white women rushed forward to stomp on his head and chest to scream insults." (Apel, 20) This story inserts this "white mob" narrative along with this image of hundreds of white bodies. They are gathered as if they were in concert or at a church visiting for a special occasion. These were images that validated artwork as in the following work which is entitled "This Is her First Lynching"

where a young white girl is being lifted by an older white woman, who looks to be happy, smiling (Wood, 232). They are surrounded by a heap of white folks looking and gazing at the lynching in their town. One may have assumed they were at a fireworks show. This was of the norm in certain communities all over the country, even though statistically, of course, it was in the south where most lynchings took place.

The two post cards on the on page 12 includeds at the top of the page, an unknown male African American, location unknown, sometime around 1900 and the postcard image on the bottom includes Jesse Williams lying on the floor. These black men were burnt, barbequed, beaten, scorched, charred, both physically and mentally. Black bodies were at the disposal of white hands any time of their choosing. So we must ask why? And how did these disturbing images impacted black communities?

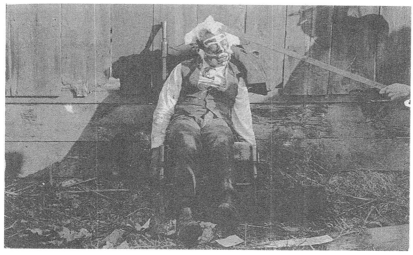

Lynchings usually proved an efficient means of intimidation and oppression. The postcard images on page 13, is from a phenomenal book, *Without Sanctuary* and is of a charred torso of an african american male hung in a coastal Georgia swamp. (Wood, 185) On the back the message reads: "Warning, The answer of the Anglo-Saxon race to black brutes who would attack the womanhood of the south!"

This was a common theme in the south, to protect the sacred body of the white woman. This was a common case of maintaining sexual roles. White men hated everything about a black man lusting, loving or assaulting a white woman. They felt it was their duty to protect them by proceeding with violence and lynchings. (Wood, 186) This included for even the slightest hint or suggestion of even the slightest transgression as ultimately was the case of 14 year old Emmett Till, discussed below.

Black communities were put into fearful situations consistently impacted by mobs of white people and the government, but after world war II the fight for enfranchisement increased (Apel, 168). Thousands upon thousands of black folks volunteered to fight for America, in hopes for freedom, in hopes of full "citizenship." However, as usual, this equal "right to citizenship" was a myth. When soldiers came back from fighting for their country, Blacks were still being a lynched spectacle, Blacks with the help of NAACP fought for their rights to stop being disenfranchised, but faced many obstacles in the 1940s and 1950s (Wood, 74-76). Dora Apel questions the government's involvement in her critique of another famous lynching book, *Without Sanctuary*, a book and exhibition divulged in the examination of these "odious social rituals." (Apel, 9) She points out there was a missing link with "the deliberate refusal of the federal government to intervene after decades of lynching and its documentation by the NAACP and other organizations, except under situations of civil disturbance or mass national protest." (Apel, 19) But because blacks of all classes were becoming more politically actively involved and bold, especially immediately after the Emmett Till case hit the international headlines (Wood, 266). Perhaps now, in the United States, it was time "to return this immense postcard to its sender!"

Emmett Till, a 14 year old boy, murdered on August 28, 1955, was the first black lynched body televised on national and international news because his mother, Mamie Till Bradley wanted to "let the world see" what was done to her son. (Apel, 179) Ultimately, she put the pressure on the United States Government to change and fix these lynchings with reaction from all over the world.(Wood, 267) The Till family evoked "an international pressure" by showing the real imagery and representations of how "america" handled Blacks in their own country. This decreased the moral standing of the U.S. and its own credibility when, post world war II, and the founding of the United Nations, America was campaigning for human rights issues worldwide, especially after the War, partially justified, by the allies involvement in fighting for the rights of other races, e.g., Jews and others who had become scapegoats in racist Nazi Germany. It began to look like the pot calling the kettle black, especially with America's denial of its own vocal extreme right, pro-German, Nazi elements, including the KKK, leading capitalists such as Henry Ford, celebrities, such as aviation hero, Charles Lindbergh, as well as all those supporting Jim Crow in America, that had been active forces in U.S. politics for years. How could America judge other countries for their lack of compassion towards one race or ethnic group, when they still allow Black bodies to be burned and made a spectacle of in their own backyard.

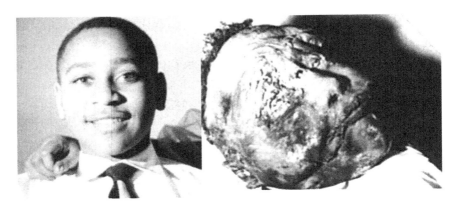

There was an influx of headlines describing how a fourteen-year-old black males mutilated body was found in the river. The description varied but had a consistent theme of him being found with a seventy-four-pound cast-iron cotton gin tied around his neck with barbed wire, he had been shot at close range, had massive injuries to his skull indicated that he was struck with a heavy instrument like an axe or heavy flashlight, his neck was still attached to the fan, parts of both ears were missing and the back of his head was practically separated from each other (Apel 179-180) This image, the most immense postcard ever, swept the world by storm. Never had the importance of "seeing" the unbearable been so effective in animating public reaction and turning a "community" affair into a national one. (Apel, 180) However, this situation even became more problematic when the killers were let loose with no conviction, and no accountability for the white man's behavior. Black people and white people based upon a "shared grief" marched for equal rights, people boycotted buses, restaurants so that it would impact white economies to show that there was value in the black community both economically and psychologically (Allen, 23).

In conclusion, black bodies were of little value to white communities, as we can see in the images shown and discussed throughout this paper. Even though, white folks meant to keep these lynching postcards within their communities, it was "too good" just to keep it a secret, they had to share with family and friends. They wanted to leave a souvenir, a cherishing moment of time. White supremacy is vivid in these images and their romanticized fetish with burning black bodies, something a normal person would have a hard time doing. However, terrorism is terrorism and some people will fall into this category. This paper was written with the hope not to cause anger, but to bring about awareness to various oppressed and non-oppressed communities so that people can see the answer to the question Apel proposed " did this really happen in the United States?" and the answer is, Yes!

Bibliography

Allen, James and Hilton Als, Congressman John Lewis, Leon Litwack. 2000. *Without Sanctuary: Lynching Photography in America.* Twin Palms Publishers.

Apel, Dora. 2004. *Imagery of Lynching Black Men, White Women and the Mob.* Rutgers University Press

Apel. D and Shawn Michelle Smith. 2007. *Defining Moments in American Photography - Lynching Photographs.* University of California Press.

Mathur, Saloni. 2007. *India by Design: Colonial History and Cultural Display.* The University of California Press.

Powell. Richard. 2002. *Black Art: A Cultural History.* Thames & Hudson Ltd. London.

Wood, Amy Louise. 2009. *Lynching and Spectacle : Witnessing Racial Violence in America, 1890 - 1940.* The University of North Carolina Press

https://www.google.com/search?q=postcards+celebrating+lynchings&biw=1200&bih=649&tbm=isch&tbo=u&source=univ&sa=X&ved=0ahUKEwjznazyq-_PAhXoilQKHVdQAAUQ7AkINg&dpr=1.2#imgdii=HIi1SYs3opSBYM%3A%3BHIi1SYs3opSBYM%3A%3BUTbdjUS2uNdx2M%3A&imgrc=HIi1SYs3opSBYM%3A

http://yalebooks.com/book/9780300063110/white-black

http://siarchives.si.edu/history/exhibits/postcard/postcard-history

http://law2.umkc.edu/faculty/projects/ftrials/shipp/lynchingyear.ht
ml - An estimated 3,445 blacks died at the hands of lynch mobs
between 1882 and 1968.

http://law2.umkc.edu/faculty/projects/ftrials/shipp/bibliography.ht
ml

ACKNOWLEDGEMENTS

First and foremost, I thank Jesus Christ, my Redeemer, Friend and Savior. I have learned to keep God FIRST in all that I do. And not religion! It is all about relationship.

To my mom/grandmother/everything Geraldine Cromwell, R.I.H. (rest in heaven) My queen. To my dad/grandfather Herbert Cromwell R.I.H. funny, stubborn and crazy man whom I owe a lot.

To my Pastors and First Lady, big brother and sister, Darrell and Roshunda Dorris. To my foster mom, Verneitte Dorris. I was lost after I lost my mom, y'all saved, cared for, guided and protected me.

My brothers, sisters, aunts and cousins- Tameka Green (Meme), Anthony Ross (Chuck/Ant) , Richard Elder (Lil Rick), Oliver Carter (Deon), Gerald Green Jr, Dionna Elder, Myesha Curry- Richardson (My), Julius Frierson(Lamar), Charles Albritton (Cj), John Frierson-Cromwell (Jon) Dominique Thompson (Dominique), Brittney Garret, Aunt Gina (Jackie) Thompson, Aunt Kelly Cromwell and Aunt Tracey Cromwell. I thank each and every one of you.

To my foster family, Brigette Dorris, Marcus and Kimberly Dorris, and Lee and Antoinette Dorris, Janice Moore, Christopher Moore and Demetrica Aubry.

And to my pride and joy, my adopted children- my nieces and nephews - Raenisha Parks, Scipio Mundine (Rashaad/Shaad), Brianna Dorris (Bri), Malcolm Aubry, Asia Lee Herron, Darrell Dorris Jr. (DJ), Divine Herron, Darius Dorris, Elijah Herron, Darion Dorris, Malik Aubry, Mecca Herron, Heather Aubry, Kaitlynn Carter Little James,

Tristan Green, Oliver Carter Jr (DJ), David Payne Jr (Little David), Marcus Dorris Jr (Markie), Mehki Dorris (Khi Khi), Lee Dorris III (Chess), Aniyah Dorris, Langston and to the one on the way, unnamed…. I love y'all.

To all of my UCLA, Mt. Sac and LFC, family, friends, my mentors Dr. Marcus Hunter, Liesel Reinhart, Dr. Pedro Noguera, Dr. Tyrone Howard, Eboni Shaw, Lindsey Goldstein, Youlanda Copeland Morgan, Michelle Johnson, Tremeal Bradford, Benny Blades, Dion Raymond, Terriel Cox, Brianna Harvey, Tunette Powell, Dante Taylor, Antwann Michaels, Debanjan, Brian Feliciano, Monica Rangel, Rohan, Jason, Liang, my best friends - Terrell, Lawrence, Tay, Rashon, Sahar, Amye, Jessica Lee, Manny, Sully, Jules, Shayla, Denae, Key, Devin and my godfather Jerry, Nikki Rocker, Bobby Grace, Chelsea Dormevil, Deavine McDaniel, Sayron Stokes, Heather Adams, Linda Diaz, Danny Cantrell, alongside with faculty, professors, colleagues that this book would not allow me to list. If you rock with me, then you know who you are!

I love you all, with all of my heart. Because of you all, I know my worth… Priceless!

ABOUT THE AUTHOR

lder Christian D. Green is a servant, Youth and Young Adult Pastor, community leader, philanthropist, innovator, entrepreneur, author and advocate. Born in a prison cell to an incarcerated mother and an unknown father, Christian has overcome many obstacles rare, atypical and uncommon to others.

Being raised in the legal custody of his grandparents, he was forced to move all over California. Born in San Bernardino, CA, then moved to Fresno, CA at the age of 4 until they decided to move to Lancaster, CA at 12 years old. Losing his grandmother at 15 years old turned Christian's life upside down and caused him to act out and neglect his educational goals.

After battling with self and realizing there was more to life than what he was experiencing, Christian decided furthering his education was necessary. He attended five different community colleges from all over California. Christian then received his Associate of Arts in Psychology from Mount Sacramento Community College (Mt. Sac) in 2014, while also traveling internationally and nationally competing on their award winning Speech and Debate Championship Team.

Immediately after graduating from Mount Sac Community College, Christian attended UCLA. While there he served on many boards and student organizations. He served as President of Black Graduate Student Association and the Organizing Director of the Graduate Student Association. He also worked heavily with the transfer community and was an advocate for all Black and other marginalized communities.

Christian graduated spring 2016 from UCLA with a Bachelor of Arts in Sociology and a minor in African American Studies. Immediately after graduating he re-enrolled as a Double Bruin at UCLA in African American Studies Department. He received his M.A. spring 2018.

Christian's current goal is to continue to serve and help in various community and student organizations in the greater Los Angeles Area. It is his endeavor to help those that are considered underprivileged or underserving to plan for their future and be the successful person God has ordained them to be since birth!

To assist him in continuing to press forward, Christian reminds himself of something Malcolm X once said, "The Future belongs to those who prepare for it today!" He also meditates on Jeremiah 29: 11, *"For I know the plans that I have for you," declares the LORD, "plans to prosper you and not to harm you, plans to give you hope and a future."*

Christian currently resides in Los Angeles CA.

Follow Christian on Instagram @christian423
Email: uncoveringyourworth@gmail.com

Made in the USA
Monee, IL
15 February 2022

90471056R00085